East
Renfrewshire
COUNCIL

Return this item by
the last date shown.

Items may be renewed
by telephone or at
www.eastrenfrewshire.gov.uk/libraries

SECRETS
OF THE
ROYAL FAMILY

SECRETS
OF THE
ROYAL FAMILY

CYRUS SHAHRAD

ARCTURUS

ARCTURUS

Arcturus Publishing
26/27 Bickels Yard
151–153 Bermonds
London SE1 3HA

Published in association with
foulsham
W. Foulsham & Co. Ltd,
The Publishing House, Bennetts Close, Cippenham,
Slough, Berkshire SL1 5AP, England

ISBN: 978-0-572-03327-9

This edition printed in 2007
Copyright © 2007 Arcturus Publishing Limited

British Library Cataloguing-in-Publication Data: a catalogue
record for this book is available from the British Library

Printed in China

CONTENTS

INTRODUCTION

The history of the British Isles is riddled with plague and fire, beset with civil strife and peppered with war and invasion. Through it all, however, the institution of the monarchy has prevailed – albeit with the occasional grisly dynastic takeover and plenty of royal infighting – providing its people with both an international profile and a figurehead of national unity and identity.

The former may have diminished over the last few centuries (it has been a long time since the sovereign personally led their soldiers into battle), but the latter seems as true now as ever before.

Despite a point in the late 1990s when the very public disintegration of royal relations seemed on the verge of bringing the House of Windsor to its knees, the Queen is finally enjoying almost unprecedented popularity levels – a sign, perhaps, that in a present made turbulent by international crises the Royal Family, for all its faults, provides an almost unbroken link with the past.

And what a past it is: from the early Viking invasions and the legendary Battle of Hastings to the cultural expansion of the Tudors, the incendiary civil collapse that split the Stuarts and the mechanized wars that put the modern monarchy to the test.

This book will expose the forgotten secrets behind that same past through a series of highly revealing chapters.

There will be an in-depth look at what really goes on behind the gates of the various royal residences, a study of countless arcane ceremonies associated with the Royal Family and a look at the way royals throughout history have fallen foul of failed marriages, public scandals, murders and tragic death.

There will also be an insight into the various bizarre conspiracy theories surrounding the tragic passing of Diana, Princess of Wales in a Paris car accident and, lastly, a timeline charting the lives of the nation's most fascinating rulers – some of them loved, some of them loathed, but every one of them contributing to this richest of royal tapestries.

The royals have endured through the ages – overcoming civil wars, invasions and international crises

PART ONE

LIFE IN THE GOLDFISH BOWL

The Royal Family are continually in the public eye, but how much do we really know about their day-to-day lives? Each of us has our own idyllic impression of what it means to be a member of the modern Royal Family (rounds of golf with world leaders, house calls from prestigious fashion designers), but the truth is often very different.

For this reason, the following chapter offers a behind-the-scenes glimpse into the lives of Britain's most privileged family. We take a tour of the various royal residences before presenting an in-depth 'day in the life' of Her Majesty the Queen (whose diary offers less space for idle contemplation than you imagine). We then take a look at the royal corgis before examining the sporting pursuits of the royal household.

The royals also have a fleet of road, rail, air and sea vehicles available to take them to and from engagements – all of which are

profiled. We then take a look at those who wanted a taste of the royal lifestyle for themselves, no matter how fleeting, as we examine the history of unwanted visitors in the palace – from the farcical (the bewildered German tourists who accidentally camped out overnight in the palace gardens) to the downright frightening (the intruder who found his way into the bedroom of a sleeping Queen).

All of which provides an interesting insight into the limitations of privilege: life as a modern royal is certainly not all country strolls and leisurely afternoon teas with the corgis.

Life as a modern royal isn't all country strolls and afternoon teas

The gates of Buckingham Palace guard many great secrets

A Home Fit for a King

The official London residence of the British monarchy was once a house belonging to the Duke of Buckingham.

In 1762, King George III acquired the site for the princely sum of £21,000, intending to use it as a private retreat (St James' Palace was still the official royal residence).

His son, the financially extravagant George IV, took his father's plans to refurbish the palace to their illogical conclusion, allowing the renowned architect Edward Nash to run wild with the blueprints: one Racaccione marble arch alone cost £34,450 (Parliament grudgingly footed the bill after George's death, but discreetly moved the

Queen Victoria found Buckingham Palace utterly lacking in charm; most modern tourists would disagree

equestrian statue of the late king, that was intended to top it, to Hyde Park).

In an effort to replenish the monarchy's steadily draining coffers, George IV's successor, William IV, replaced Nash with the more economical Edward Blore, whose aesthetically rather humdrum designs (Queen Victoria later dubbed him 'Blore the Bore') at least allowed the palace to be completed on budget. William chose not to live there, however, and, when Queen Victoria officially moved in following her coronation in 1837, she was said to be less than happy with her new home, which was reputedly cold because of faulty chimneys, dirty due to lazy staff and reeked thanks to a problem with the ventilation.

Needless to say, such problems were
sorted out and Buckingham Palace today
is truly the most sumptuous and
spectacular of royal residences, with
sprawling royal gardens (the largest in
London), 78 bathrooms (in one of which
The Beatles claimed to have smoked a
joint before being awarded their MBEs by
Her Majesty), 92 offices, no fewer than
240 bedrooms (188 of them for the
palace's live-in staff) and 19 state rooms.

Among the last are such ornate chambers
as the Victorian Ballroom, where the
Queen confers honours and hosts her
elaborate state banquets; the Music
Room, venue for numerous royal
christenings since the palace chapel was
bombed in the Second World War; and the
Throne Room, site of royal portraits,
formal addresses and – until 1958 – the
legendary debutante balls, at which
eligible young ladies were presented to
the Queen in full court dress and with
three tall ostrich feathers in their hair.
Princess Margaret claimed the ceremony
had to be abolished because 'every tart in
London was getting in'.

*The sprawling palace grounds play host annually to
the Queen's highly popular garden parties*

Other Royal Residences

The Long Walk to Windsor Castle through Windsor Great Park, a view almost unchanged through the centuries

WINDSOR CASTLE, BERKSHIRE

During the Second World War, King George VI and his family travelled to Windsor Castle every night to avoid the German bombing raids (a closely guarded secret at the time, as the image of the royals facing the same threat as their fellow Londoners was thought to promote a sense of camaraderie). In 1992, a fire in the Queen's private chapel ravaged nine of the principal state rooms and severely damaged 100 more. In fact, Buckingham Palace was opened to the public to help finance the repairs, which took five years.

A stone's throw from Buckingham Palace, St James's Palace is currently the royal residence of Princess Anne, among others

ST JAMES'S PALACE, LONDON

Originally commissioned by Henry VIII and built on the site of a former leper hospital, St James's Palace became the principal royal residence in London following the fire that destroyed Whitehall Palace in 1698, although it steadily declined in importance following the establishment of Buckingham Palace. Nearby Clarence House, formerly home to the Queen Mother, is now the London dwelling of Prince Charles and his family.

SANDRINGHAM HOUSE, NORFOLK

Originally purchased by Queen Victoria, Sandringham was far ahead of its time in terms of modern conveniences (being among the first of such buildings to boast gas lighting, flushing toilets and even a shower of sorts). It is also a popular hunting destination: King Edward VII was so fond of shooting on the surrounding 8,000 acres that he had all the clocks there set half an hour earlier to allow him to engage in it a little longer ('Sandringham Time', as it was known, was finally abolished in 1936).

The Royal Family regularly chooses to spend Christmas in luxurious Sandringham House, often staying there until February

KENSINGTON PALACE, LONDON

In 1981, apartments eight and nine of this splendid 17th century redbrick palace – birthplace and childhood home of Queen Victoria – were combined to make a suitably luxurious London house for the newly married Charles and Diana; indeed, it remained the latter's official residence until the day of her death.

The black wrought-iron gates of Kensington Palace became obscured by an enormous drift of floral tributes following the tragic death of Diana in 1997

The Power and the Glory

The age-old question of what it is the Queen actually 'does' within the chambers of her various royal residences is one that has intrigued tourists for generations.

More than 50 years of meeting the people has given the Queen a talent for informal public engagements that most aspiring politicians would kill for

The image of an elderly lady firing off orders to her minions and shaping national policy between meals is an attractive one indeed, but largely inaccurate: the Queen still wields some of the weightiest executive powers in the country (including the ability to declare war, dismiss the Prime Minister or dissolve Parliament), but these are largely formalities and the majority of her policy work is simply a case of giving the royal nod of approval to decisions already made by her cabinet.

In addition to her role as Head of State, the Queen occupies other senior positions – including Head of the Commonwealth, Supreme Governor of the Church of England and Head of the Armed Forces. Yet it seems fair to say that the lion's share of her day-to-day work relates to her more symbolic role as head of the nation – an immediately identifiable icon, and embodiment of national ideals and focus of British unity.

As such, one of her weightiest responsibilities is to see and be seen by as many of her subjects as possible, thus instilling in them a sense of historical significance and purpose. To this end, she has received over three million letters since her accession in 1952, welcomed well over a million guests to her famous summer garden parties and made no fewer than 256 official visits to 129 separate countries – hardly nine-to-five work in the conventional sense, but a full-time job nonetheless.

Her Majesty's Diary

From the minute she wakes until the moment she turns out her bedside light, the Queen is on duty as Head of State and the Commonwealth – a duty carrying with it a seemingly endless number of responsibilities, although it is certainly not a hard life in the traditional sense, as this typical diary day goes to show.

7.30am

The Queen is woken by a chambermaid bringing her morning tea on a silver tray, the milk for which comes directly from the royal cattle at Windsor Castle. While enjoying her tea, Her Majesty's wireless is tuned to BBC Radio 4's news and politics show, *Today*.

8.30am

Takes breakfast in the first-floor dining room with her husband, Prince Philip – generally cornflakes or porridge, served not in a bowl but in one of her favourite Tupperware containers.

9.30am

Meets her private secretary, Robin Janvrin, for a briefing on the day's events – mostly visiting public institutions, opening new buildings and conferring honours upon outstanding citizens (nearly 400,000 such honours have been given out since her accession in 1952).

1.00pm

If still in the palace, the Queen usually prefers to take lunch alone – although she may have a page call for one of her children to join her: an occasion giving rise to strictly formal greetings despite the familiar company (a curtsey and a kiss from her daughter Anne, or a bow and then two kisses – one on the hand and then one on the cheek – from her sons Charles, Edward or Andrew).

If still in the palace, the Queen usually prefers to take lunch alone – although she may have a page call for one of her children to join her

20

*The Queen's duties include honouring not only national but also international figures.
Here, Microsoft founder and noted philanthropist Bill Gates is awarded an honorary knighthood in
2005 – although the fact that he isn't British means he can't use the title 'Sir'*

2.30pm

Weather permitting, the Queen takes a walk in the sprawling palace gardens, during which time everyone except the palace gardeners is expected to make themselves scarce. No one may speak to Her Majesty unless she addresses them first.

3.00pm

The rest of the afternoon is dedicated to the Queen's social duties – usually overseeing the roughly 620 organizations and charities of which she is patron, although the summer months tend to be dominated by preparations for the famous garden parties in the palace grounds.

6.30pm (Wednesdays only)

The Queen holds her weekly private audience with the current Prime Minister to discuss affairs of state, a highly sensitive engagement at which no one else is present and of which no PM has ever discussed the details. Tony Blair is the only British premier ever to have had the gumption to cancel the royal briefing in favour of more pressing business – Her Majesty, by all accounts, was not amused.

7.30pm

Her husband returns from his own business and the couple enjoy a drink in their private apartments (Her Majesty's tipple of choice is vermouth, an aromatic fortified wine), after which Prince Philip often goes out once more and leaves the Queen to dine alone in front of the television, her supper on a silver tray. After dinner, the Queen likes to indulge her penchant for popular crime writers (she lists PD James, Dick Francis and Agatha Christie among her favourites) or, at the end of the week, attempt the notoriously difficult crossword in the British *Sunday Times* newspaper.

Attending public events with her husband Prince Philip is a regular fixture in the Queen's diary

11.00pm

The Queen retires to bed, although her light often stays on for another hour or so while she sifts through the last of the day's paperwork, traditionally brought to her in a series of red boxes.

In the Doghouse

Few humans can claim to have enjoyed the Queen's affections in the way her troop of well-turned-out corgis can: indeed, her clan of Pembroke Corgis – numbering four at any given time – holds a special place in Her Majesty's heart and an almost free rein in the palace grounds.

Corgis were originally brought to Wales by marauding Vikings (*cor gi* means 'dwarf dog' in Welsh), although Her Majesty's own are almost always descended directly from Susan, the corgi given to the Queen on her 18th birthday (Susan was stowed in the back of the carriage – unbeknown to her new husband Philip – on their honeymoon). Since then, these canines have become almost as established a part of British culture as the Queen herself, as the following facts show:

The Queen's clan of Pembroke Corgis – numbering four at any given time – holds a very special place in Her Majesty's heart

⚜ In 2002, the popular children's novelist Dick King-Smith wrote *Titus Rules!*, the fictional adventures of the Queen's favourite corgi, who is seen attending to all manner of mishaps in the royal household – from catching burglars to putting out fires.

⚜ The Queen also has three 'dorgis': corgis crossbred with dachshunds. The royal photographer Norman Parkinson was reputedly once bold enough to ask how the short-legged dachshund was capable of mating with the taller corgi, and was told by Her Majesty: 'Oh, it's quite simple. We have a little brick.'

⚜ In 1999, a royal footman named Matthew King was demoted after it transpired that he had been spiking the drinking water of the royal corgis with whisky and gin for the amusement of his colleagues, who enjoyed watching them drunkenly bumping into things.

Few dogs enjoy so pampered an existence as the royal corgis

In 2003, one of the Queen's corgis, Pharos, had to be put down after its legs were badly mauled by an English Bull Terrier owned by Princess Anne, leaving the Queen inconsolable. Less than a year earlier, Princess Anne had found herself fined £500 and given a criminal record (the first for a member of the Royal Family) after the same dog, Dotty, attacked two children in Windsor Great Park.

It is hardly a dog's life for the royal corgis: each has its own Christmas stocking, plus rubber booties to protect their paws from the gravel outside the Palace and wicker baskets equipped with stilts to protect them from draughts.

Sport of Kings

For members of the British monarchy, being able to engage in all manner of sports is one of the perks of the job – although some do so with more success than others. Here we examine a few of the preferred royal pursuits.

HORSE RACING

The Queen herself is an avid racing enthusiast, regularly forsaking the daily papers over breakfast to scrutinize the pages of the *Racing Post*. Nor is her interest merely academic, keeping an eye as she does on the breeding of her own horses and then enthusiastically championing them at various national races throughout the year, often with real success (at the 1957 Royal Ascot, for example, she had four winners in one week).

The Queen's life may seem sedate to the casual onlooker, but the thunderous rush of the races is a thrill of which she never seems to tire

*Golf has long been a popular royal pursuit – here Prince Charles
tees off on a trip to New Zealand in 1994*

GOLF

Prince Andrew has taken a late interest both in playing golf (he boasts a handicap of five) and promoting it, although his attempts at the latter recently landed him in hot water with conservationists, who were enraged by his plans to team up with American businessman Donald Trump and build a £1 billion golf course on a Scottish nature reserve. Nor is this the first time golf has landed the royals in trouble: in 1991, Prince William was admitted to the Royal Berkshire Hospital in Reading with a depressed fracture of the forehead after a friend accidentally hit him with a golf club at a nearby golf course.

SKIING

Prince Charles and his family have long been accomplished skiers, regulars at the upmarket Swiss resort of Klosters. The association with this chocolate box Alpine town hasn't always been so tranquil, however: in 1988, Charles was lucky to escape death when his off-piste ski party triggered an avalanche, which claimed the life of his closest friend, Major Hugh Lindsay, former equerry to the Queen, and left another friend, Patti Palmer-Tomkinson, needing to be resuscitated at the scene. Charles was among those digging with his bare hands to free his friend following the slide.

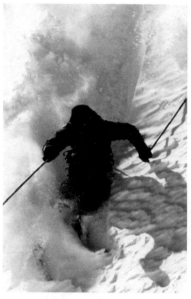

Skiing is among the most dangerous sports on earth, a fact that fails to dampen royal enthusiasm

ETON WALL GAME

This rather muddled hybrid of rugby and soccer has been a tradition at William and Harry's former public school since 1766. The game is so arcane the rules look like they're being made up as they go along, with a wallside scrum called a 'bully', a touchline called a 'calx' and with goal scoring so notoriously difficult that on average one is claimed every ten years. Prince Harry was an enthusiastic player and in 2002 led his team to victory during the annual St Andrew's Day match, by far the most important fixture of the year.

HUNTING

The royal association with blood sports has long been a bone of contention with animal rights activists. In 1926, the Queen's father, George VI, killed an African elephant with 90lb (41kg) tusks and was later quoted as saying that he felt very lucky, 'as there are not many big ones left'. His own father, George V, was such a hunting enthusiast that on one trip to Nepal he managed to bag 21 tigers, eight rhinos and one bear, although contemporaries claimed that the whole event was stage managed to ensure that his victims had no chance of escape. More recently, Prince Philip tried to divert his grandchildren William and Harry following the death of their mother, by taking the boys for regular stag shoots on the sprawling Balmoral Estate.

Big game hunting and shooting would be frowned upon for a modern monarchy

'Home, James!'

Waiting aimlessly for delayed public transport is a torment the royals rarely have to endure, thanks to the fleet of road, rail and air vehicles on hand to whisk them across the country – or the world – to their various public duties.

The Queen inspects a custom-made Bentley presented to her as a gift during her Golden Jubilee celebrations in 2002. The car is specially modified to withstand bullets and bombs

STATE CARS

The Royal Mews at Buckingham Palace is home to eight state cars purpose-built to ferry the Queen to and from engagements both in and out of the country. The convoy

consists of two Bentleys, three Rolls Royces and three Daimlers, all painted in royal claret, with a silver icon featuring a horse-bound St George that is removed and affixed to whichever car is being used at the time. The Queen also has the privilege of being the only person in Britain who is allowed to drive without registration plates of any kind. These days, the Queen is most usually seen in her purpose-built Bentleys, which feature tailor-made, rear-hinged doors that allow the Queen to be fully standing before she steps out into public view – a sure way to avoid embarrassing trips or falls.

ROYAL CARRIAGES

For occasions demanding a different kind of horsepower, the Royal Mews also houses over 100 historic and highly decorative horse-drawn carriages, many of which are still used in ceremonial processions today. The most famous of these is the Gold State Coach, which has been used at the coronation of every British monarch since George IV in 1821 (it was actually built for his father, George III, but wasn't ready in time for his own accession). At 12ft (3.6m) high, 23ft (7m) long and weighing over four tons, it is no surprise that a team of eight horses is required to pull the Gold State Coach, the surfaces of which are resplendent in gold leaf, ornamental painted panels and elaborately sculpted figures and animals.

THE ROYAL TRAIN

Along with sleeping, dining and office carriages – all painted in the traditional royal claret – the Royal Train also includes the Queen's Saloon and the Duke of Edinburgh's Saloon, both of which contain en-suite bedrooms, bathrooms and sitting rooms, with the last also boasting a decorative piece of the original broad gauge railway designed by Isambard Kingdom Brunel. Incidentally, Brunel accompanied Queen Victoria and Prince Albert on the first ever royal train journey in 1842 – a 25-minute trip from Windsor to Paddington that greatly pleased Her Majesty, although Albert was reputedly left rather pale by the experience ('Not quite so fast next time, Mr Conductor,' he said upon disembarking).

THE ROYAL YACHT BRITANNIA

At 125m in length, weighing 5,769 tons and with a main mast topping out at 42m, the Britannia was a suitably luxurious vessel, boasting room for 250 guests, plus a crew of 19 officers, 217 Royal Yachtsmen and a captain with the rank of commodore, none of whom were allowed to shout orders at each other (a complex system of hand signals was instead used to keep things civil). Britannia was finally decommissioned in 1997 after clocking up no less than 1,087,623 miles; she now operates as a floating museum and conference centre from her permanent mooring in Leith, Edinburgh.

AIR TRAVEL

The short-reigning King Edward VIII was the first monarch to be a fully qualified pilot and it was he who founded what was then known as the King's Flight in 1936 to provide air transport for all royal trips. The accession of Elizabeth II in 1952 saw it renamed the Queen's Flight and the acquisition of its first helicopter, a Westland Dragonfly, with her husband, the Duke of Edinburgh, becoming a qualified pilot the following year. The Queen's Flight was officially disbanded in 1995 and its duties transferred to Royal Air Force division No.32 (The Royal) Squadron, which operates all royal flights on BAe 146 or HS 125 jet aircraft, although there is also a Sikorsky S-76 C+ helicopter at the disposal of the royal household. These flights are operated by the royal household from Blackbushe Aerodrome in Hampshire.

Inside and outside views of the opulent Royal Yacht Britannia, decommissioned in 1997, much to Her Majesty's obvious dismay

An Intruder in the Palace

With such a lavish lifestyle, it is perhaps unsurprising that many of us might feel a pang of envy when reading about the trappings of the Royal Family. But there are those who decided to act on those feelings and endeavoured to see for themselves what royal life is all about – if only for a fleeting moment.

On July 9th, 1982, the Queen woke to find an Irishman in his early thirties perched on the edge of her bed, one hand lacerated and dripping blood onto the bedsheets, the other clasping the jagged remains of a shattered glass ashtray.

The man, whose name was Michael Fagan, had scaled the fortified 14ft (4.25m) walls at 6am before breaking into the palace (twice setting off an intruder alarm, which was twice silenced by the guard on duty, who thought it was malfunctioning). He then wandered around the palace halls, admiring a few paintings (even reputedly greeting a palace housekeeper) and accidentally breaking the glass ashtray, lacerating his hand in the process. Not long after, he found his way to the Queen's bedroom.

Upon waking, the Queen was forced to hold Fagan in conversation for more than ten minutes, managing to trip the intruder alarm only after he asked her for a cigarette. The unemployed father of four was then subdued by staff and arrested, although he escaped conviction in favour of a three-month recuperative spell at a renowned mental hospital.

Nor was Fagan the only person to have evaded security.

1837

A 12-year-old boy known only as the Boy Cotton manages to spend almost a year living rent-free in Buckingham Palace, hiding in the chimneys and blackening the sheets of whichever spare room he chose to spend the night.

Despite stringent security measures, unwelcome intruders have been a part of palace life for centuries

1941

The Queen Mother surprises a British army deserter hiding in her private bathroom at Windsor Castle. She reputedly gives him a lecture on the importance of national service before calling security and sending him packing.

1972

An armed man named Ian Ball attempts to kidnap Princess Margaret outside Buckingham Palace, firing six shots from a parked car before he is wounded by return fire and then chased down by her bodyguard, James Beaton (who later receives the George Cross for his efforts).

1981

Three German tourists scale the walls of Buckingham Palace and camp out overnight in the royal gardens, apparently under the misapprehension that they are in Hyde Park. They are not evicted until the following morning, when they wander up to a bemused security guard and ask for directions to the exit.

1994

The notorious American prankster James Miller paraglides onto the roof of Buckingham Palace, where he then parades around naked save for a coating of green paint and some glow-in-the-dark highlights on his private parts. The palace is evacuated and Miller subsequently arrested and banned from the UK for life on the grounds of 'flying without a ticket of air worthiness'.

2003

The self-styled 'comedy terrorist' and Edinburgh fringe performer Aaron Barschak manages to break into Prince William's 21st birthday celebrations at Windsor Castle despite being visibly inebriated and wearing the costume of a cross-dressing Osama bin Laden. He then staggers onto the stage during William's speech and kisses the prince on both cheeks before sauntering off to the bar, where he is arrested by security.

The Queen Mother: seemingly unfazed by strange men lurking in her bathroom, she was more concerned with making sure that London's children were cared for during World War II

PART TWO

COURTLY TRADITIONS

The worldwide fascination with the British Royal Family owes much to its association with ancient history and nowhere is this more apparent than in the seemingly endless list of arcane traditions that it refuses to lay to rest (the surreal practise of Swan Upping, for example).

In this chapter, we'll be looking at the historical customs that underpin and inform the Royal Family. How, for example, does one act in the presence of Her Majesty?

How much money does the Queen actually make and where does it come from? What role do knights of the realm play in the modern world and what does a person have to do to become one?

How much money does the Queen actually make in a year and where does this large amount of money come from?

We'll also be looking at some of the more obscure job descriptions in the royal household, examining the monarchy's most eccentric characters and offering an in-depth breakdown of some brilliantly bizarre royal ceremonies. We'll finish off with a look at the coveted crown jewels – and how they were very nearly stolen.

There is no way to account for every custom surrounding the British Royal Family, but the following at least provides an insight into its complex relationship with the conventions of days gone by.

The distinctive bearskins and tunics form an integral part of the charm of Changing the Guard, perfomed like clockwork every day during the summer, and every other day for the rest of the year

Meeting Her Majesty

She may be no larger or more intimidating than the average grandmother, but coming face to face with the Queen can be a nerve-racking event – not least because of the seemingly endless number of dos and don'ts that constitute 'royal protocol'.

Things have been relaxed in recent years, with officials insisting that there are no formal codes, only points of common courtesy. Put a foot wrong, however, and you're likely to incur the wrath of a nation, as former Australian Prime Minister Paul Keating found out in 1992 when he was photographed with his arm around Her Majesty – an action that earned him the nickname 'the Lizard of Oz' among his British detractors.

Familiar touching of the Queen is, in fact, among the most cardinal of sins: traditionally, men execute a neck bow with the head only, while women are expected to curtsey (Cherie Blair, wife of the British Prime Minister and a fierce anti-monarchist, has come under repeated fire for her own half-hearted efforts). Hand shaking is permitted, but it is better to wait until the royal hand is extended than proffer your own and find it ignored.

Nor are the guidelines concerning what to call the Queen any less stringent: the first time you address her, it should be as 'Your Majesty' and 'Ma'am' (as in 'jam', not 'farm') each time thereafter.

Other points of etiquette to bear in mind when in her presence include:

Never show the Queen your back, and try not to leave the room before she does.

Hats are acceptable, but should be restricted to social functions after 6.30pm. Gloves should be removed before meeting the Queen.

When writing formally to the Queen, letters should open 'Madam' and end 'I have the honour to be, Madam, Your Majesty's humble and obedient servant'.

If you're inviting the Queen to luncheon (and bear in mind that she gets over 1000 such invitations each year), meals should be limited to three courses and go on for no longer than one hour and 45 minutes.

Frank Sinatra showed impeccable decorum when presented to Queen Elizabeth at a movie premiere in 1958

A Right Royal Farce

It is hardly surprising, what with all the public attention and pressure to embody outmoded ideals, that so many royals display characteristics that can be called eccentric at best and endearingly loopy at worst.

Take Prince Charles, who seems determined to involve himself in all manner of scientific and environmental issues. In 2004, the media had a field day when Charles weighed into a complex debate on nanotechnology by expressing his fear of a future dominated by a race of 'nanomachines' reducing everything in their path to 'grey goo'. He has also been lampooned in the past for having admitted to talking to his plants and – as a child – singing to seals from the cliff tops of Caithness in Scotland (the traditional song *Over The Sea To Skye* got the best reaction, apparently).

It is his personal demands upon staff, however, that have caused the most uproar. He is reputedly so fussy about his boiled eggs that palace cooks are forced to make seven at a time, after which they are tested for consistency by the prince himself and the best one selected. Personal aides are also believed to have been submitted to tasks such as squeezing toothpaste on to the royal toothbrush and – when Charles was suffering with a broken arm – having to hold a specimen jar in place.

Prince Charles is reputedly so fussy about his boiled eggs that palace cooks are forced to make seven of them at a time

As embarrassment over his marriage to Diana begins to diminish, Charles is once again enjoying a hallowed place in the hearts of the British people – not least because of his often delightfully eccentric behaviour

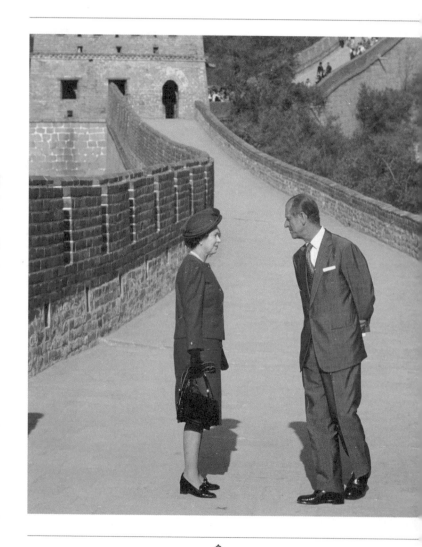

Whatever foibles Prince Charles may boast, they pale when compared to the behaviour of his father, Prince Philip.

Despite being revered as a reincarnated deity by an obscure South Pacific tribe on the Island of Vanuatu (he ignored their request for a photograph of himself wearing nothing but a traditional grass penis sheath), most Brits consider the Duke of Edinburgh to be a bit of a 'blunderbuss'.

His regular gaffes are a source of constant embarrassment for palace officials (and amusement to the media), as the following quotes amply testify.

'You are a woman, aren't you?'
(To a Kenyan woman who had presented him with a gift, 1984)

'If you stay here much longer, you'll all be slitty-eyed.'
(To a group of British students on a state visit to China, 1986)

'Aren't most of you descended from pirates?'
(To a native of the Cayman Islands, 1994)

'Do you still throw spears at each other?'
(To a group of Australian Aborigines, 2002)

'It looks as if it was put in by an Indian.'
(Pointing to an outdated fuse box while touring a factory in Edinburgh, 1999)

This picture of the Queen and Prince Philip atop the Great Wall of China was taken on the very same visit, in 1986, on which the Prince made his infamous 'slitty-eyed' remark

45

The Price of Royalty

Those in favour of abolishing the monarchy regularly point to the amount of money it is granted by the Government. At the same time, officials are keen to stress that the royals are pursuing a more streamlined, 'modern' approach to their finances, doing away with many of the luxuries taken for granted by their successors and cutting corners where necessary.

The retirement in 1997 of the Royal Yacht Britannia, for example, may have caused some anguish for the Queen, but it was a necessary step in proving the Royal Family could economize; the same is true of reducing travel on the Royal Train, which costs an estimated £35,000 per journey, or on private flights, which work out at £8,000 per hour (848 hours of flight time were accumulated between 2004 and 2005).

But perhaps there is a limit to what a a member of royalty should be expected to give up. Prince Charles, for example, spends an estimated £2 million a year on such outgoings as grooms, chefs and gardeners at Clarence House. Are these reasonable expenses for a man in his position or personal extravagances?

Royal officials were pleased to announce in 2006 that Her Majesty had cost the average British taxpayer just 62p for the previous year. With a British population of more than 60 million, that gives the royal household £37.4 million a year of taxpayers' money to use. The debate continues.

Royal trips such as this visit to Canada in 2005 (the Queen is pictured here alongside Alberta Premier Ralph Klein) don't come cheap – the royal plane alone costs £8,000 per hour

While the Queen herself carries money only once a week (a folded note – of unknown denomination – for the church collection box each Sunday), she owns just a fraction of the Royal Collection of art and heirlooms, and in 1993 agreed to pay a certain (albeit limited) amount of income tax. Her personal fortune is rumoured to be in excess of £275 million. This is largely thanks to the way in which money accumulates from her private estates, including Balmoral and Sandringham (both inherited from her father), and the sprawling Duchy of Lancaster –18,800 acres of land and assets dating back to Henry IV's accession in 1399.

The Queen's personal fortune is rumoured to be in excess of £275 million. This is largely thanks to the way in which money accumulates from her private estates

BALANCING THE ROYAL BOOKS

The bulk of palace funding breaks down into three main categories, each of them granted annually by Parliament.

❧ The Civil List
£7.9 million (of which the Duke of Edinburgh receives £359,000) to help the Queen fulfil her role as Head of State and Head of the Commonwealth.

❧ Property Services Grant-in-aid
Put towards the maintenance of the royal residences and constituting £14.3 million in 2005–06.

❧ Royal Travel Grant-in-aid
Used to offset the cost of royal travel, particularly private flights and journeys on the expensive Royal Train (the cost of travelling by state car is covered by the Civil List). £5.9 million was allocated for the year 2005–06.

Cost cutting has led to a certain amount of tightening of the royal purse strings, but this picture of the Queen's birthday celebrations in 2005 shows she is still capable of travelling in style

Who Says Chivalry is Dead?

Alongside lesser recognitions of national contributions, the Queen continues to confer knighthoods as the ultimate acknowledgment of services to British society, with everyone from actors and athletes to music stars like Tom Jones and Mick Jagger having received this most coveted honour.

Knighthoods, which are conferred at investitures held 20 times annually in the ballroom of Buckingham Palace (and once a year at Holyrood Palace in Edinburgh), carry no military obligations whatsoever, but link the bearer to a tradition of gentility dating all the way back to the Middle Ages, while granting

Francis Drake is knighted by Queen Elizabeth I after becoming the first Englishman to sail around the world; the ceremony itself remains largely unchanged to this day

them the title 'Sir' (for men) or 'Dame' (for women).

The custom of inaugurating a knight remains much the same today as it has been for centuries, with the recipient kneeling before the Queen as she lays the blade of her sword first on one shoulder and then the other, thereafter bidding them stand while she invests them with the insignia of their new order. There are also other orders that the Queen may bestow upon her subjects:

THE MOST DISTINGUISHED ORDER OF ST MICHAEL AND ST GEORGE
Established: 1818

Motto: *Auspicium Melioris Aevi*
(Token of a better age)

Founded to honour British diplomats for contributions to the State or Commonwealth in foreign nations, the order includes three classes. Ian Fleming had his famous creation, James Bond, appointed CMG (the lowest class) in his classic novel *From Russia With Love* (1957).

THE MOST NOBLE ORDER OF THE GARTER
Established: 1348

Motto: *Honi soit qui mal y pense*
(Shame on him who thinks this evil)

This most ancient and prestigious of chivalric orders, inaugurated by King Edward III, may claim no more than 25 living members at any one time. Inaugurations take place at the church service held each June in St George's Chapel, Windsor Castle.

THE MOST EXCELLENT ORDER OF THE BRITISH EMPIRE
Established: 1917

Motto: *For God and the Empire*

As the most junior chivalric order, this is also the one that boasts the most members, although its links with colonization have caused controversy in the past: in 2003, the Rastafarian poet Benjamin Zephaniah publicly rejected an OBE because of its association with 'years of brutality'.

Symbols of Royal Power

Few things stir the souls of patriotic Britons like the opening bars of their national anthem, *God Save The Queen*, the effect of which testifies to the awesome power embodied by the monarchy and its ability to inspire through symbolism alone.

It is for this reason that punk band The Sex Pistols' anarchical *God Save The Queen* ('God save the Queen / Her fascist regime') touched such a raw nerve upon its release in 1977, a few weeks before Elizabeth II's Silver Jubilee. On the official jubilee holiday, June 7th, the band members were arrested while trying to perform the song on a Thames barge floating outside the Palace of Westminster. The monarchy was understandably horrified by the song, but it made it to number two in the official UK singles chart nonetheless (many claim that it was deliberately kept off the top spot to avoid offence), thus making the band international superstars almost overnight. Early A&M 7inch versions of the single now change hands for over £13,000, making them among the most valuable records of all time.

It is not just through the national anthem, however, that royal authority makes itself felt; various icons are used

to convey the power of the Queen across the world, some of which are examined here.

The Sex Pistols rub salt into the wounds by signing their contract with A&M Records outside Buckingham Palace in 1977 – much to the displeasure of the local constabulary

Royal Warrants

Granted to companies that have provided goods or services to the Royal Family and thereafter displayed as a sign of excellence. Among those marked for honour are Aston Martin (cars), Burberry (clothing), Twinings (tea) and Fortnum and Mason (groceries), although the cigarette company Benson and Hedges had its royal warrant removed in 1999.

A coin bearing the profile of Queen Victoria, facing in the direction tradition demands

Coins

The tradition of having English rulers represented on coins dates back to the 8th-century monarch King Offa, although it was his successor Alfred the Great who introduced the first mints. Since the reign of Charles II, custom has dictated that monarchs are depicted on their coins facing in the opposite direction to their predecessors – a custom broken by Edward VIII, who wanted to be depicted facing to the left because he felt it was his 'better side'.

The Royal Standard

Following Princess Diana's death, the public was horrified that there was no flag flying at half mast above Buckingham Palace. But back then the only flag ever displayed there was the Royal Standard and only then as an indication that Her Majesty herself was on the premises (that subsequently changed and the Union Jack is now flown at all other times). The Royal Standard is made up of three lions passant to represent England, one lion rampant representing Scotland; and a harp to symbolize Ireland: it is also flown on state cars and even planes (when grounded), but never at half mast, a sign that there is always technically a living monarch.

Stamps

The first mass-produced adhesive postage stamp was the now highly collectible Penny Black, featuring the face of a young Queen Victoria, which went into circulation on May 1st, 1840. Modern stamps, meanwhile, feature a portrait of Queen Elizabeth II originally designed as a sculpture by Arnold Machin in 1967 and now believed to be the most widely reproduced piece of art in history thanks to the more than 150 billion copies made.

The Queen herself has travelled to 129 countries; her image has visited many more

Odd Jobs

There is only one Queen, but beneath her there are some 1,200 employees making up the royal household at any given time – and some of them fill positions that are unusual to say the least. Here we take a look at some of the more interesting.

Ladies-in-Waiting

The official title of any woman attending upon female members of the royal household, although those personally serving the Queen herself are formally known as Women of the Bedchamber. The most senior lady-in-waiting is known as the Mistress of the Robes – a position traditionally filled by a duchess, although she is usually only ever called upon at state ceremonies.

Gold Stick

Bodyguard to the royal household with responsibility for the personal safety of the sovereign, the office of Gold Stick dates from Tudor times, although the role has been largely ceremonial since the reign of Queen Victoria. Gold Stick's deputy, perhaps unsurprisingly, is known as Silver Stick.

Princess Anne was Gold-Stick-in-waiting at the State opening of Parliament in 2001

The Royal Greenwich Observatory, established in 1675 by Charles II. The 'time ball', visible on top of the building, drops each day at 1pm exactly

Astronomer Royal

For a traditional salary of £100 per year, the Astronomer Royal is on hand to advise the monarch on all matters space-related – a position first established by Charles II, who also set up the Royal Greenwich Observatory in 1675. The current Astronomer Royal, John Rees, is something of a controversial figure, having previously espoused theories of balloon-like alien life forms and – in his book *Our Final Century* – the possibility of humans being wiped out by a race of super-intelligent machines.

Master of the Queen's Music

A position that has its roots in the court musicians of the Middle Ages, these days it constitutes a single classical composer charged with writing music to accompany occasions of royal or state significance. Previous incumbents include Sir Edward Elgar (1924–34), who wrote *The Nursery Suite* for Princesses Elizabeth and Margaret in 1931, and Sir Arnold Bax (1942–53), who composed Elizabeth II's Coronation March.

Poet Laureate

Like the Master of the Queen's Music, the poet laureate is charged with composing works to celebrate royal or state occasions, in exchange for an honorary stipend of £200 and a supplementary barrel of sherry. Noted poet laureates have in the past included Nahum Tate (1692–1715), who shame-lessly cobbled together a less gloomy ending to Shakespeare's *King Lear*, and Alfred, Lord Tennyson (1850–92), who wrote *Charge of the Light Brigade* to commemorate the Crimean War.

Domestic music-making at the palace in 1842. Prince Albert plays the organ for Victoria and composer-conductor Felix Mendelssohn, at this time the toast of London

Queen's Piper

Personally responsible for playing 15 minutes of bracing bagpipe music beneath the Queen's window every weekday morning; during state banquets, he also coordinates the 12 pipers playing around the dinner tables. The position was officially inaugurated by Queen Victoria after she was taken with the personal piper of the Marquess of Breadalbane during a visit to Taymouth Castle in 1842.

Warden of the Swans

See page 64.

To the untrained ear, the sound of Scottish bagpipes can seem inexplicably tuneless, but it is served as a stirring royal alarm clock for over 150 years

Pomp and Circumstance

Steeped as they are in centuries of tradition, royal ceremonies are notoriously high in symbolism – and none of them more so than the annual State Opening of Parliament by the Queen, who inaugurates the political year with a speech from her throne in the House of Lords in Westminster.

First of all, a detachment of the Yeoman of the Guard searches the cellars beneath the Houses of Parliament for explosives – a custom dating from the failed Gunpowder Plot of 1605 (see page 132).

The Houses of Parliament, scene of some of the strangest ceremonies in the royal calendar

At the same time, one Member of Parliament (MP) is held 'hostage' in the halls of Buckingham Palace to guarantee the safe return of the monarch, a tradition rooted in the days when sovereigns enjoyed less than amicable relations with the policy makers at Westminster.

The same is true of the theatrics surrounding the speech itself, which calls upon the man known as Black Rod (named after his unique ebony staff) to usher MPs from the democratically elected House of Commons into the unelected House of Lords. The first time he knocks on the door to the Commons, it is slammed back in his face as a symbol of the Commons' political independence; the second time he raps three times with his staff, responding to the call 'Who is there?' by shouting 'Black Rod', after which the MPs file in for the speech.

All of which may seem rather pointless (not least because, theoretically, if she wanted to, the Queen could dissolve the entire Parliament), but then, when it comes to royal ceremony, the more colourful and, to modern eyes at least, convoluted the better.

Changing of the Guard

A ceremony (11.30am daily from April to July; alternate days for the rest of the year) that sees one set of guards end their vigil outside Buckingham Palace and another take their place. The clockwork marching of the guards – dressed in full uniform including towering bearskin hats – is accompanied by music from a military band.

The Changing of the Guard never fails to delight tourists with its mix of flawless marching, charming uniforms and traditional military music

Trooping the Colour

An elaborate military march performed three times every June – the first two as rehearsals for the third, which marks the Queen's 'official birthday' (her actual birthday, in April, is deemed too likely to be rained off). The Queen used to take part on horseback herself (once being forced to regain control of her steed after a 17-year-old boy fired six blank shots at her during the parade), although since 1986 Her Majesty has taken part in the event from the safety of Queen Victoria's ivory-mounted phaeton.

Maundy Thursday

A ceremony in which the sovereign distributes alms to the poor on the Thursday before Easter. The practice is rooted in the biblical story of Jesus washing the feet of his disciples at the Last Supper (in the 14th century, King Edward III used the occasion to personally wash the feet of the poor), although these days Her Majesty simply distributes small red and white purses containing specially minted Maundy Money, the value of which (in British pence) matches the Queen's age at the time.

When Trooping the Colour, the horses have to be as sure of their steps as the soldiers – one mistake, and the whole thing is thrown

They have little to worry about now, but it was not so long ago that London's swans lived in danger of landing on the royal dinner table

Swan Upping

The surreal practice of Swan Upping dates back to the 12th century, when all unmarked swans on the River Thames were the property of the sovereign and thus regularly eaten at elaborate state banquets. The five-day ceremony still takes place every June – with the royal Warden of the Swans and Marker of the Swans setting off in skiffs to symbolically 'claim' the Queen's swans – although these days the practice has a purely conservational purpose and no animals are eaten.

Coronation

The form of the royal coronation has been virtually unchanged for more than a thousand years, with the incoming king or queen taking the royal oath and then being anointed in King Edward's Chair (made in 1296) by the Archbishop of Canterbury (since the coronation of George II in 1727, this has been done to the tune of Handel's *Zadok the Priest*). Elizabeth II's own coronation, on June 2nd, 1953, saw revellers across the country taking to the streets despite the pouring rain; it was also the first royal coronation to be shown on television, much to the horror of traditionalists, including Sir Winston Churchill.

The imposing facade of Westminster Abbey has for centuries watched men and women enter its doors as mere mortals and leave as kings and queens

The Crown Jewels

The degree of security surrounding the crown jewels in the Tower of London makes the thought of stealing them hard to entertain, but that is exactly what was going through the mind of Irish-born Colonel Thomas Blood in 1671.

The Tower of London continues to provide a seemingly impenetrable fortress for the coveted crown jewels

After spending several weeks befriending the Tower's resident jewel keeper, Talbot Edwards, Blood managed to secure a private viewing for himself and two of his friends – one of whom then knocked Edwards out with a mallet, and gagged and stabbed him. The three then set to work: one man filed the Sceptre with the Cross in two and stashed it in his clothes; another stuffed the Sovereign's Orb down his trousers; and Blood himself flattened St Edward's Crown with the mallet and hid it under his coat.

At that point, their luck ran out, as Edwards' son burst on to the scene and sounded the alarm. The men were arrested before they had made it beyond the Tower walls – although Charles II later publicly pardoned Blood, a fact that caused many to speculate that the King himself had staged the bungled burglary with the aim of selling off the jewels and patching up some of the holes in royal finances.

The jewels on display today are the same ones almost pilfered by Blood

Engraved for Chamberlain's History of London

Blood and his Accomplices.
Escaping after stealing the CROWN from the TOWER.

Stealing the Crown Jewels: an act that was rumoured to be the plan of Charles II

and his band, created for the coronation of Charles II (the original crown jewels were dismantled, sold and melted down for coinage by Cromwell). They include various swords, orbs and sceptres (the Sceptre with the Cross, for example, was created in 1611 and modified in 1905 to bear the 'Great Star of Africa', the largest diamond in the world at 4oz (106g)), as well as numerous crowns, of which the following overleaf are notable examples.

Imperial State Crown (1937)

The most elaborate of all British crowns, used at the close of royal coronations and the State Opening of Parliament. The Imperial State Crown contains no fewer than 2,868 diamonds, 273 pearls, 17 sapphires, 11 emeralds and, at its centre, the chicken-egg-sized Black Prince's Ruby, dating back to 1367 and worn in a gem-encrusted helmet by Henry V at the legendary Battle of Agincourt.

St Edward's State Crown (1661)

A replacement for the original coronation crown of Edward the Confessor and still used to crown new monarchs (although both Queen Victoria and Edward VII chose to avoid it because of its unprecedented 4lb 12oz (2.16kg) weight). This is the same crown hammered flat by Captain Blood, although it has since been fully restored and, in 1911, was set with 444 semi-precious stones.

The Imperial State Crown is the most elaborate of all British crowns

Small Diamond Crown of Queen Victoria (1870)

This was commissioned by Queen Victoria, who by 1870 had been persuaded to return to public life following a protracted period of mourning for her late husband, Albert, but who refused to wear the Imperial State Crown because it wouldn't fit over her mourning veil. This small silver crown was therefore created and embellished with 1,187 diamonds taken from a necklace belonging to the Queen herself.

Queen Victoria wearing the unconventionally dainty diamond crown for which she is best remembered

PART THREE

FAIRYTALE BEGINNINGS

Royals throughout history have struggled to seek out spouses displaying the important characteristics of good breeding and match with whom would bring political benefits. True love was a luxury that few royals could afford.

There is also the added pressure of the intense public scrutiny: the expectation generated by a ceremony as spectacular as Charles and Diana's wedding in 1981 created a sense that its stars were fairytale sweethearts when they were, of course, mere humans, probably thrown together by forces beyond their control. When royal marriages begin to fall apart – as so often they do – the gory details are dissected in sensationalist tabloid newspapers.

In this chapter, we'll be looking at some of history's more notable royal couplings, with a retelling of Edward VIII's scandalous marriage to the American Wallis Simpson and Prince Charles' weddings to both Diana Spencer and Camilla Parker-Bowles. There'll also be an insight into the meaning of the term 'blue blood', a look at Prince William's taste in women and the bizarre history of Henry VIII's six wives.

Queen Victoria marries Prince Albert in 1840; the pair would later prove to be a truly happy couple

King Edward VII's marriage, in 1863, to the Danish Princess Alexandra

Star-Crossed Lovers

For many people, the idea of a king passing up the throne in favour of the woman he loves is the very essence of a fairytale romance, but when it actually happened, in 1936, it was a disaster from which the monarchy only barely recovered.

The king in question was Edward VIII, who as a handsome young Prince of Wales had cultivated a reputation as a notorious playboy with a string of mistresses. It was at a high-profile party held in 1931 by one such mistress, Viscount Thelma Furness, that Edward first met Mrs Wallis Simpson, the twice-married American actress who was to change the course of his life and thus shape history itself.

Simpson's past was hardly the stuff of a suitable royal match; Americans were looked on unkindly in 1930s Britain and her family, while respectable, was far from distinguished. She had divorced her first husband, a US Navy pilot, following his post-war descent into alcoholism, marrying Ernest Simpson, heir to a family shipping business, six months later.

Ernest was attending the party at which the prince and Mrs Simpson first met, but he was pushed ever further into the background over the course of subsequent years, during which time the young lovers saw increasingly more of each other. Things came to a head in August 1934, when the pair found themselves united on a cruise that Wallis's husband was unable to attend – a cruise on which, Wallis later stated, she and the prince 'crossed the line that marks the indefinable boundary between friendship and love'.

Edward's dashing character fooled Britain into thinking he would make a formidable king

Edward with the woman who stole his heart – and who almost brought an entire nation to its knees

The price of love

He may have captivated the British people, but Edward became a reluctant and ill-fitting king following his father George V's death on January 20th, 1936. His regular lateness and general lack of enthusiasm for state affairs made him unpopular with his ministers, who mumbled secretively about the effect of their new sovereign's infatuation on his ability to rule competently. Soon after, Edward received a letter saying that the government was on the verge of resigning unless the king gave up his common mistress, forcing him to make the difficult decision between love and leadership.

It wasn't a decision that Edward dallied over. At 10am on December 10th, 1936, the king signed the mandatory six copies of the formal Instrument of Abdication. The following day, Edward broadcast a speech to the nation in which he said: 'I have found it impossible to carry the heavy burden of responsibility and to discharge my duties as king as I would wish to do without the help and support of the woman I love.'

The kingship thus passed onto his brother Albert, while Edward had to content himself with the title His Royal Highness the Duke of Windsor; Wallis, when they married at a small ceremony in June 1937, became Duchess, but the Royal Highness

BLUE BLOOD

Edward VIII's relationship with Wallis Simpson was scandalous for the simple reason that it broke with centuries of tradition demanding that English monarchs marry a consort of good breeding, thus perpetuating the purity of the royal line and preserving what is known as 'blue blood' within the family.

The results are occasionally close-knit enough to border on the overly familiar; Prince Philip, for example, is the Queen's second cousin once removed on his father's side and her first cousin twice removed on his mother's, while Charles and Camilla are ninth cousins once removed through Camilla's great grandmother, Alice Frederica Edmonstone Keppel, who was King Edward VII's mistress from 1898 until his death in 1910.

Like father, unlike son: Edward and George V, in whose enormous shadow he cowered

title was his alone, and was not permitted to pass on to his children.

The couple were thereafter shunned by the royals and British society in general, living out the rest of their days as exiles in France (save for a short period during which Edward served as governor of the Bahamas). Albert, who had chosen to reign under the name George VI, had them removed from the Civil List and paid Edward's allowance personally; Edward reputedly called his brother to beg for more money on an almost daily basis in the first days of his reign, after which the calls were disconnected. The price of love, it seems, was expected to be paid in full.

Such problems are deemed a small price to pay, however, in the wider effort to tie the Royal Family back to the first English kings, although this becomes rather a fanciful idea once the various domestic uprisings and international takeovers are accounted for – from the Norman Conquest to the dynastic succession of the German Hanoverians in the early 18th century.

Then there is the issue of legitimacy to account for: various onlookers assert that Prince Harry's irregular red hair is proof that he is the offspring of Diana's extramarital affair with her riding instructor, James Hewitt – and if it could happen at the tail end of the 20th century, then who is to say how much the royal bloodline has been diluted throughout history?

Three's a Crowd

In 1995, Diana shocked the world by speaking openly to the BBC about her life with Prince Charles. 'There were three of us in this marriage,' she said, 'so it was a bit crowded.'

Her comment, an attempt to justify her own adulterous relationship with her riding instructor, James Hewitt, was an allusion to her husband's ongoing infidelities with long-term mistress Camilla Parker-Bowles. Charles and Camilla (nee Shand) had met at a polo match in 1970; the chemistry was obvious and instantaneous, but their relationship was discontinued and three years later Camilla married Andrew Parker-Bowles.

It wasn't long, however, before Charles was orchestrating elaborate trips to Germany, in his capacity as Colonel-in-Chief of the Royal Regiment of Wales (now the Welsh Regiment), to engage in illicit weekend flings with

Charles never managed to extinguish his feelings for Camilla, despite it being she that nudged him in the direction of Diana

Camilla at the military base in Osnabruck, where she was ostensibly 'visiting relatives'. The affair continued long after Charles' own marriage to Diana in 1981; the lovers bought each other presents, had affectionate pet names for one another (Fred and Gladys, a nod towards their mutual love of the BBC radio comedy *The Goon Show*) and regularly spoke at length on the phone.

A transcript of one such sexually explicit conversation was published by a tabloid newspaper in 1993, leading to a very public crescendo in what had become known as 'the War of the Waleses' since their separation the previous year. And while the couple's subsequent divorce allowed Diana to put the crushing formality of palace life behind her and lead a more normal life, including several relationships, it brought Charles back to the arms of the only woman he'd ever really loved: Camilla Parker-Bowles.

'The War of the Waleses' culminated in the publication of an explicit phone conversation between Camilla and Charles in 1993

The fact that 20,000 well wishers turned out to congratulate Charles and Camilla on their wedding day in 2005 suggested that the couple's past infidelities had been largely forgiven

A new beginning

In February 2005, Charles and Camilla's wedding date was formally announced as the following April 8th, although it ended up being pushed back by 24 hours to allow the Prince of Wales to attend the funeral of the recently deceased Pope John Paul II.

Not that the couple seemed particularly upset – after years of negative public exposure, a degree of privacy was exactly what they wanted. The union itself was to take place at an informal civil ceremony – the first royal wedding in history to do so, a fact that caused no end of legal issues and an announcement that the Queen, as Supreme Governor of the Church of England, would be unable to attend.

She was, however, present at the subsequent church service and hosted the reception, both held in the castle. Despite an initial reluctance to welcome Camilla into the family, the royal blessing appeared finally to have been given – a fact seemingly confirmed by the diamond engagement ring, a Windsor family heirloom that had once belonged to the Queen Mother.

The public, too, seemed largely to have accepted Camilla. Crowds began lining the streets of Windsor at dawn on April 9th, with 20,000 cheering the couple as they arrived amid heightened security (unnecessary save to subdue one enthusiastic male streaker) to tie the knot.

Charles and Camilla eventually left for their honeymoon in a Bentley decorated by Princes William and Harry, with the words 'Prince' and 'Duchess' sprayed on either side. Camilla had become heir to the consort's throne and the second highest ranking woman in Britain after the Queen, but it was felt that her official title, Princess of Wales, was too closely associated with the late Diana and would upset the public if adopted; as a result, the Duchess of Cornwall would have to do.

Charles and Camilla left for their honeymoon in a Bentley decorated by William and Harry

A Fairytale Wedding

Despite the fact that the British public grew more or less accustomed to the idea of Charles' second marriage – going so far as to compliment the oft-maligned Camilla's unexpected sense of style on the big day – it was hard not to draw comparisons between this largely overlooked civil ceremony and the fairytale spectacle of Charles' wedding to Diana, which had the whole world's undivided attention on July 29th, 1981.

Charles and Diana tied the knot at St Paul's Cathedral in front of 3,500 invited guests, with 600,000 spectators lining the streets of London to pay their respects to the young couple and more than 750 million watching the ceremony on television, making it the most popular television programme ever broadcast.

Diana, just 20 at the time, travelled from Clarence House to the ceremony in the traditional Glass Coach with her father, Earl Spencer. Walking up the red-carpeted aisle of St Paul's itself took her more than three and a half minutes, wearing as she was an elaborate silk dress with a 25ft (7.6m) train.

Both parties were nervous enough to slightly fluff their lines when it came to the exchange of vows: Diana muddled the order of Charles' forenames, calling him Philip Charles Arthur George (rather than Charles Philip), while Charles accidentally promised to share with Diana 'thy goods' instead of 'my worldly goods'.

After taking an open-top carriage back to Buckingham Palace, the newlyweds appeared on the ceremonial balcony and dispensed with royal protocol to give the public what they'd been waiting for all along – a truly royal kiss, which appeared on the front pages of papers around the world the following day.

The seemingly happy couple's flawless smiles gave no indication of the heartbreak yet to come

A partnership of equals for Prince William?

As the future King of England, potential applicants for Prince William's hand in marriage are understandably not in short supply. Add to this the fact that he is a rather dashing lad with a solid academic record, inherent athleticism and an adult life thus far divided between charity work and military service, and the appeal of 'Dreamboat Willie' becomes all too obvious.

As such, he has had an endless string of admirers, from weak-kneed school girls (off limits at Eton thanks to a set of rules, laid down by the Queen, that included 'no kissing') to celebrities like the pop star Britney Spears, who admitted in 2002 to having been stood up by the prince after initiating a string of flirtatious emails.

It wasn't until January 2006, however, that William appeared finally to have set his sights on a suitable love interest, ending years of media speculation by publicly kissing his girlfriend Kate Middleton, a former housemate from his days at St Andrew's University, whose attendance at various royal functions (not to mention an appearance on a Windsor family ski trip to the Swiss retreat of Klosters) seemed to suggest that she had the approval of the Queen as well as the prince himself.

Prince William has had an endless string of smitten admirers – from weak-kneed school girls to celebrities like the pop star Britney Spears

William has attempted to dispel rumours of an impending engagement, but already various merchandise companies in the UK are busily preparing for a run of commemorative William and Kate wedding memorabilia. And why not? Kate has thus far proven herself a model girlfriend, smart and suitably pretty and displaying a surprising decorum at even the most intimidating of formal functions.

The fact that she has been invited skiing in Klosters implies that Kate has the royal nod of approval

The Many Wives of Henry VIII

The meltdowns of recent royal relationships pale into insignificance when compared to one king who changed his country's laws to pursue the woman he wanted. A man of voracious appetites in more ways than one, the larger-than-life Tudor King Henry VIII is perhaps best known for having taken no less than six wives during his long and prosperous reign – only half of whom lived to tell the tale.

Henry VIII boasted an unfortunate appetite for short-lived marriages – and wives

CATHERINE OF ARAGON
(married 1509, divorced 1533)

Catherine's inability to bear a son was her undoing

The Catholic daughter of King Ferdinand and Queen Isabella (founders of the Spanish Inquisition), Catherine was originally married to Henry's brother Arthur, who died in 1502, six months after their wedding. She subsequently married Henry, but was unable to bear him the heir he desired, suffering a miscarriage and producing a stillborn daughter, two sickly sons that died in infancy and finally a daughter, the future Catholic Queen Mary. By this point, Henry was in love with one of his wife's attendants, Anne Boleyn, and so began his unsuccessful petitioning of the pope for an annulment of his marriage to Catherine. When Anne fell pregnant, he dissolved the power of the pope and established himself as head of the new Church of England, divorcing Catherine on his own authority.

ANNE BOLEYN
(married 1533, executed 1536)

Legend describes Anne as being afflicted by everything from prominent moles to a sixth finger on one hand, but she was clearly desirable enough to enchant the disillusioned king (17 of his passionate love letters to her remain locked in the Vatican Library), not to mention wily enough to demand that he promise to make her his queen before giving in to his advances. And yet her

Anne's execution was Henry at his harshest

pregnancy – trumpeted to the point that the word 'Prince' had already been written on the proclamation of birth – turned out to be yet another daughter, the future Queen Elizabeth I, born in September 1533.

Desperate to reassert herself in Henry's eyes, Anne fell pregnant twice more during the following two years, but miscarried both times. Henry's eye, meanwhile, had fallen on one of her ladies-in-waiting, Jane Seymour, and so he had Anne tried and eventually executed on trumped-up charges of adultery along with several of her friends, family members and accused lovers, some of whom were tortured to extract confessions and then hung, drawn and quartered.

JANE SEYMOUR
(married 1536, died 1537)

Some say that Jane truly loved the king; others claim that she responded to his advances out of fear for her own life. Either way, within 24 hours of Anne Boleyn's execution the two were formally betrothed. In 1537, she fell pregnant, eventually giving

Jane truly won the heart of her king

birth to a son, Edward. Complications with the birth left Jane much debilitated and she died a few weeks later. Henry had her body installed at his own tomb in St George's Chapel, Windsor, with the result that she is the only one of his wives to actually be buried beside her king.

Henry VIII has been seen as everything from a model king to a barely repressed woman hater

ANNE OF CLEVES
(married January,
divorced July 1540)

Henry remained single for more than two years after Jane's death, suggesting that he may have been genuinely affected by her passing. After this, however, it became clear that a solid political marriage was needed – the previous two having been love matches and thus contributing nothing financially or in terms of international allies – and so Henry began sending diplomats to scout out the loveliest ladies from various foreign courts.

The royal painter, Hans Holbein, had been dispatched to Cleves, and his portrait of the Duke's sister Anne so enchanted

Henry that he agreed to a marriage on the strength of the picture alone. When he finally met her, however, he was less than impressed, referring to her as his 'Flanders Mare' and looking for a way out of the marriage even as it was taking place in 1540. Anne eventually accepted his demand for an annulment of the union on the grounds that it had not been consummated, knowing full well that her life depended on it.

KATHRYN HOWARD
(married 1540, executed 1542)

In keeping with a by now well-established tradition, Henry had fallen for one of Anne's courtiers in the dying throes of their ill-fated marriage. He married Kathryn

To marry Henry VIII was to risk death; to cheat on him was to virtually guarantee it

Howard just 16 days after formally separating from Anne; he was 49, she was just 19.

Henry, it would seem, dearly loved his new wife; she greatly eased his violent mood swings – brought about by his increasing obesity and incapacitation from an ulcerated leg – and he in turn referred to her as 'a rose without a thorn'. Kathryn's desire for company of her own age, however, was her undoing; she had various admirers in the palace (even being young and foolish enough to engage one as her private secretary) and, when rumours of her repeated infidelities finally reached the king's ears, he flew into a rage and had her executed in the Tower.

KATHERINE PARR (married 1543, died 1547)

The daughter of a modest country squire, Katherine had been twice widowed when she was finally married to the king on July 12th, 1543, 18 months after the execution of Kathryn Howard. Henry's health had declined so much by this point that her role was more that of a full-time nurse than a wife, but she greatly endeared herself to the royal court with her piety and became extremely close to the king's children. Katherine eventually outlived Henry, who died on January 28th, 1547.

Katherine's piety and care melted the dying king's heart

Romances Through the Ages

The various clauses and conditions governing the selection of a suitable consort have ensured that British history is thick with mismatched couples and royal infidelities – although there have, of course, been plenty of happily married kings and queens. Here we examine some of the most notable (if not always entirely successful) pairings of the past.

EDWY THE FAIR (955–959)

Appeared to spend as much time addressing affairs of state as he did indulging in the bedroom charms of his mistress (later his wife) Elgifu, who was in fact the daughter of his mother-in-law (also another of his mistresses) Ethelgive – both factors that made their relationship highly unpopular in Edwy's court.

EDWARD THE CONFESSOR (1042–1066)

Too pious even to consummate the marriage to his beloved wife Eleanor, Edward died childless and thus without an obvious heir, leading to the succession crisis that saw William the Conqueror usurp the throne and the Normans take over the English ruling class for centuries to come.

Edward the Confessor's decision to remain chaste may have been morally upstanding, but his failure to produce a viable heir threw England into turmoil

WILLIAM RUFUS (1087–1100)

William's homosexual tendencies were reflected in the company he kept: the chronicler William of Malmesbury describes a royal court flooded with 'effeminate' young men wearing 'shoes with curved points'; Orderic Vitalis notes a prevalence of 'fornicators and sodomites'. Perhaps unsurprisingly, William Rufus never married.

EDWARD I (1272–1307)

Edward was so devastated at the death of his wife, Eleanor, who had borne him no fewer than 16 children, that he erected 12 elaborate stone sculptures – the 'Eleanor Crosses' – to mark the points at which the funeral cortege would stop overnight on its passage from Lincoln to Westminster Abbey. Three still stand (Waltham Cross, Northampton and Geddington) and there is a 17th-century replica outside Charing Cross Station in central London.

Edward may well have been a romantic but he was also capable of defending himself and his loved ones from attack – he fought off an assassin who hoped to kill him as he slept

Edward III, whose relationship with Alice Perrers would soil his legacy for centuries to come

EDWARD III (1327–1377)

Following the death of his wife, Phillippa, in 1369, Edward took a mistress, the notorious Alice Perrers, who shared his bed with her daughter. Edward lavished gifts upon her (including jewellery once belonging to his late wife); Perrers, in return, is rumoured to have stolen the rings off his fingers when he died.

RICHARD II (1377–1400)

Richard was so distraught when his wife, Anne, died at Sheen Palace that he had the entire building razed to the ground.

EDWARD IV (1461–1483)

One of very few kings to marry for love and get away with it, Edward wed the beautiful widower Elizabeth Woodville at a secret ceremony attended only by the bride's mother and two ladies-in-waiting.

CHARLES II (1660–1685)

Charles died without siring a single legitimate heir, but himself acknowledged no fewer than fourteen illegitimate children by at least seven separate mistresses, including the rags-to-riches orange-seller-turned actress and society girl, Nell Gwynne, whose mother ran a

From pauper to actress to the darling of high society, Nell Gwynne was often mentioned in Pepys' diaries. Mistress of Charles II, and having previously been the mistress of Charles Hart and Charles Sackville, she jokingly entitled the king her 'Charles the Third'

brothel and who herself may have worked as a child prostitute.

GEORGE IV (1820–1830)

In 1795, George was introduced to the short, overweight and apparently filthy Caroline of Bruswick, a woman he had previously agreed to marry. George, who went pale at the introduction, is reputed to have asked the Earl of Malmesbury for a glass of brandy. He subsequently drank solidly until the day of the wedding itself, the evening of which found him so inebriated that he collapsed into the fireplace of the bridal suite and stayed there until morning.

VICTORIA (1838–1901)

The death of Prince Albert in 1861 plunged Victoria into such a deep depression that she retired almost entirely from public life and wore black until her dying day. That said, she did enjoy an unusually close relationship with her outspoken Highland servant, John Brown, and rumours that the two entered into a secret marriage later in her life persist to this day – rumours bolstered by the fact that she asked to be buried with his picture and a lock of his hair.

PART FOUR

RIGHT ROYAL SCANDALS

The days when the Divine Right of kings assured that what happened inside the palace stayed inside the palace are long gone. The modern age of zoom lenses, investigative journalists and online forums has seen the privacy of the Royal Family all but eradicated, with countless domestic indiscretions becoming front-page news in the name of public interest.

The morality of media intrusion is a subject of endless debate, but many argue that privacy is the price one pays for living a life of unparalleled privilege and luxury. After all, the royals are held up as models of society – surely there can be no skeletons in the cupboard of this most straitlaced of British families?

The royals are held up as the very models of society – surely there can be no skeletons in the cupboard of this most straitlaced of British families?

Throughout the 20th century, the royals have time and again proved themselves to be as human as the rest of us thanks to a long list of social scandals. In this chapter, we'll be examining some of the most notable, from the Queen's infamous *Annus Horribilis* and the secret life of her sister, Princess Margaret, to the various controversies surrounding Prince Edward's embattled business plans. There'll also be profiles of outspoken Princess Michael of Kent, royal wild-child Prince Harry and Diana's much-maligned former butler, Paul Burrell, among many others.

In recent times, it has been the antics of Prince Harry that have caught the media's attention

The Worst of Times

On November 24th, 1992, the Queen Elizabeth used her speech at London's Guildhall to declare the previous twelve months 'not a year on which I shall look back with undiluted pleasure. In the words of one of my more sympathetic correspondents, it has turned out to be an *Annus Horribilis*.'

The correspondent in question was the late Sir Edward Fox, erstwhile Private Secretary to the Queen, who was referring to the catalogue of disasters that had befallen the Royal Family in 1992; from the very public separation of Princes Charles and Andrew from their wives to the divorce of Princess Anne and – just days before the speech itself – the fire that raged through Windsor Castle, leaving up to £40 million worth of damage in its wake.

Prince Andrew and Sarah Ferguson

Diana is herself believed to have played the role of matchmaker in bringing Prince Andrew and Sarah Ferguson together in 1985. The Duke and Duchess of York were married at an elaborate ceremony in Westminster Abbey a year later, and 'Fergie' initially found herself taken into the hearts of the British public at large; a sprightly character who smiled in all the right places and whose bright red locks lent some much needed colour to the notoriously stuffy royal establishment.

Queen Elizabeth before her infamous 'Annus Horribilis' speech at London's Guildhall in 1992. Many remarked at the time that her choice of black clothing suggested a woman in mourning for a year in which everything that could have gone wrong seemed to have done exactly that

The year 1992 turned out to be the Queen's Annus Horribilis

Behind the scenes, however, things very quickly began falling apart. Andrew's naval duties meant that Fergie saw her husband on average for two days of every week and she was left to raise their two children Beatrice (b. 1988) and Eugenie (b. 1990) almost single-handedly, while press and public alike started mercilessly lampooning Fergie's weight problems.

The couple officially announced their separation on March 19th, 1992. Less than six months later, Fergie was snapped by the tabloids sunbathing topless with her financial advisor, John Bryan, who at one point appeared to kneel down and suck the former duchess's toes. The graphic nature of this final transgression appeared too much for the British public and Fergie's popularity plummeted to an all-time low.

It didn't help that the Duke and Duchess had been living well beyond their means, spiralling into roughly £4 million worth of debt with their jet-set lifestyle – a fact that saw Fergie put pen to paper for the first in a series of successful children's books, *Budgie*

Fergie has become a prolific columnist, campaign spokesperson (most notably for Weight Watchers) and talk-show host – even standing in for Larry King

the *Little Helicopter* (although the character was later alleged to have been copied from Arthur W. Baldwin's *Hector the Helicopter*).

Fergie's commitment to regaining her financial independence has been her saving grace. She has become a prolific columnist, campaign spokesperson (most notably for Weight Watchers) and talk-show host – even occasionally standing in for the inimitable Larry King. Indeed, the path to reinvention has seen Fergie achieve an almost cult status in the US – as her appearance in a 1998 episode of the globally popular TV show *Friends* testifies.

Fergie and her
financial advisor,
John Bryan, with
whom she was
photographed in
a compromising
position

Princess Anne and Mark Phillips

Princess Anne married army officer and former Olympic horse-rider gold medallist Captain Mark Phillips in a spectacular Westminster Abbey ceremony in 1973.

As the first of the Queen's children to tie the knot, her subsequent life on the family estate at Gatcombe Park came under intense media scrutiny, but the couple appeared in public increasingly rarely and seemed cold and unfamiliar with each other when they did. In 1989, after much public speculation and media coverage, the couple formally announced their separation due to irreconcilable differences.

Not least of these was the birth, in 1985, of Phillips' illegitimate child, Felicity Tonkin, the product of a brief fling in New Zealand. Captain Phillips initially contested the paternity suit, but was forced to concede when the results of a DNA test in 1992 proved that he was indeed the father – a duty he subsequently acknowledged by setting up a trust fund for the young girl.

By this point, Anne was deeply involved with another military man, Rear Admiral Timothy Laurence, whom she had met when he was serving as equerry to the Queen in the late 80s. The relationship caused an enormous stir in 1989, when love letters from Laurence were stolen from Anne's private briefcase and exposed in the British tabloids. On December 12th, 1992, the couple were married at a small church near Balmoral – and it seemed at last that this terrible year was destined to finish on an optimistic note.

Happiness, however, has eluded the couple, a fact that insiders blame on the Royal Family's insistence on treating Laurence – the South London-born son of a salesman – like a commoner at best and a servant at worst. As a result, Anne and Timothy are now said to be leading almost entirely separate lives.

Princess Anne married army officer Captain Mark Phillips in a spectacular ceremony

*Princess Anne and Mark Phillips seemed the epitome of young love at their
spectacular wedding in 1973, but lasting happiness was to elude them*

The Windsor Great Fire

Few events have weighed so heavily on today's Royal Family than the fire that tragically ravaged Windsor Castle at the tail end of 1992.

The blaze began around 11.30am on Friday November 20th, when a halogen lamp being used by decorators set fire to a curtain in the Queen's Private Chapel, but it spread quickly through the building's antiquated wooden interior and before long the majority of the ancient State Apartments were in flames.

The alarms were sounded and by 11.45am the first engines had arrived; by 12.20pm, the blaze was being attended by 35 engines and 200 firefighters – many of them called in from surrounding towns.

Even so, the fire raged all day, creeping into towers, collapsing roofs and incinerating various historical furnishings well into the evening, with the assembled forces only managing to gain control of the inferno around 8.00pm, and with small secondary fires burning well into Saturday morning.

Luckily, there were no serious injuries or deaths, although a 21-year-old decorator was hospitalized for burns incurred while trying to rescue valuable paintings from the chapel. Five firemen were also ferried from the scene (two with hypothermia, three with minor burns) and the official Surveyor of the Queen's Pictures suffered a suspected heart attack.

Windsor Castle's ancient wooden interior made it a veritable tinderbox when fire broke out in late 1992

The real casualty, however, was the castle itself. In total, over 100 rooms were badly damaged by the fire, many of them – including the Crimson Drawing Room, the Queen's Private Chapel and the State Dining Room – chambers of enormous historical importance. Luckily, those worst affected had been emptied of furnishings the previous day to make way for necessary rewiring, although several valuable objects and works of art were lost, including a 19th-century Henry Willis organ and Sir William Beechy's equestrian portrait of King George III.

The final cost of the fire was estimated at between £30 million and £40 million. The Queen herself personally contributed £2 million to the restoration, although the vast majority of the work, completed in 1997, was funded by the decision to open Buckingham Palace to a paying public.

The fire continued burning for almost 24 hours, causing between £30 million and £40 million worth of damage

Other Scandals

These days, royal divorces are as ingrained a part of British culture as the marriages themselves. Back in 1976, however, when the Queen's younger sister announced that she was separating from her husband, Anthony Armstrong-Jones, the nation found itself reeling from the shock.

Not least because the split coincided with the publication of 'intimate pictures' of Princess Margaret and her highly unsuitable suitor, the landscape gardener and failed pop star Roddy Llewellyn, who was 17 years her junior.

Perhaps they shouldn't have been so surprised: Princess Margaret had long been noted for her glamorous lifestyle and the wildly hedonistic parties that she hosted at her private home on the Caribbean island of Mustique. The antics on the island made headlines in the media.

Long before her marriage she had been famously serenaded by Frank Sinatra and romantically linked to a string of eligible men including Mick Jagger and Peter Sellers, the latter once going so far as to express his determination to marry the young royal.

Princess Margaret had long been noted for her rather glamorous lifestyle and the wildly hedonistic parties that she hosted at her private home on the Caribbean island of Mustique – her antics there made headlines

Princess Margaret embarks upon her ill-fated marriage to Anthony Armstrong-Jones in 1960. When the pair broke up in 1976 – the first modern royal couple to do so – the British public felt things couldn't get much worse. But then that was before they'd been introduced to her new boyfriend...

At that time, Margaret herself had eyes for one man only: a decorated Battle of Britain pilot and captain of the royal household named Peter Townsend. The fact that Townsend was a divorcee meant that there was no way the royal authorities could assent to the union, and so it was that Margaret was forced to weather her unhappy marriage to Armstrong-Jones for more than 16 years.

Following their separation, Margaret stayed with her footloose Llewellyn for eight years – years in which her stock fell to unthinkable levels among the British public, with even MPs at one point questioning whether she was worth the £75 million she received annually from the Civil List.

Eventually, the age gap drove Llewellyn into the arms of a younger woman and Margaret lived out the rest of her life alone, increasingly dependent on the bottles of Famous Grouse whisky that friends always kept to hand in case she stopped by unexpectedly. Her final years were fraught with illness caused by a life of smoking and she died following a massive stroke on February 9th, 2002.

Margaret was blessed with a dark beauty that helped cement her position as the original party princess

Prince Edward

Prince Edward's career as a TV producer didn't exactly get off to a flying start. In 1987, the Queen's youngest son persuaded members of the Royal Family to take part in a special one-off edition of the popular game show *It's A Knockout*, which pitted participants against each other in a series of bizarre physical challenges, and which saw Princess Anne, the Duke and Duchess of York and Edward himself donning fancy dress costumes while cheering on their respective teams.

The event raised over £1 million for charity, but was ridiculed in the media (Edward famously stormed out of the subsequent press conference when greeted by the titters of bemused journalists) and its comic denigration of previously untouchable Royal Family members was later considered by many to mark the beginning of the decline of royal popularity in the 1990s.

Prince Edward's forays into television production have been unsuccessful at best and downright damaging at worst

Undeterred, in 1993 Edward founded his own TV production company, Ardent, but things only went from bad to worse.

Over the following decade, the company lost money year after year, and in 2001 an Ardent production crew was accused

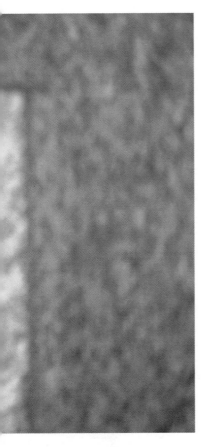

In 2001, Edward's production company Ardent was widely condemned for hounding Prince William during his first days at St Andrew's University

Clarence House had previously brokered a gentleman's agreement with the media, asking them to leave the prince alone in exchange for photos and interviews during a public 'walkabout' with his father days before term began. Only one company broke the agreement – his uncle's. Just days into freshers' week, an Ardent crew was spotted setting up cameras outside William's hall of residence and was ejected from the premises. They were also accused of taking William's fellow first-years out for an Indian meal in exchange for gossip about the young prince.

It later transpired that the crew was desperate for footage after being commissioned to produce a programme called *The A–Z of Royalty* for the US-based E! Entertainment Network. At the time of their expulsion from St Andrew's, Edward had managed to secure just one willing interviewee for the programme: his father, Prince Philip.

of invading Prince William's privacy less than a week into his life as a student at St Andrew's University in Scotland.

Princess Michael of Kent

The woman less-than-affectionately referred to by the British press as 'Princess Pushy' appears determined to make as many enemies in the papers as within the palace itself.

Princess Michael once haughtily informed an American interviewer that she had more royal blood in her veins than any person to marry into the Royal Family since Prince Philip (her Hungarian mother was descended from both a mistress of the French King Henry II and Catherine de Medici, Queen of France).

Years later, a tabloid reporter disguised as an Arab sheik tricked her into speaking openly about the late Princess Diana, whom she referred to as 'nasty' and 'strange', and nothing more than 'a womb' to her husband, Charles. She also noted that her children were the brightest and best-qualified royals of their generation.

All of this pales in comparison, however, to the PR disaster that occurred when Princess Michael found herself seated beside a group of boisterous black diners in New York's trendy Da Silvano restaurant in May 2004. Unable to contain her frustration at the volume of their voices, she reputedly marched over, slammed her fist on their table and suggested that they 'go back to the colonies'.

The diners in question, many of them high-profile media and fashion industry people, were aghast.

Princess Michael referred to Princess Diana as 'nasty' and 'strange', and nothing more than a mere 'womb' to her husband, Charles

Princess Michael's aloofness had already made her something of a pariah within the Royal Family when her racist comments caused international outrage in 2004

Paul Burrell

Few people have fallen out of favour with the British public quite so spectacularly as Princess Diana's former butler, Paul Burrell. Diana had long referred to Burrell as 'my rock'; he travelled with her around the world and provided a much-needed shoulder to cry on when palace life became too much for the young princess.

So powerful was their bond that, in 1997, it was Burrell who first dressed and applied make-up to Diana's body in Paris before it was retrieved by her ex-husband and removed to England. In November of the same year, the Queen honoured him with the coveted Royal Victoria Medal for 21 years of loyal service.

That same service became an issue of much debate on the January 18th, 2001, when Burrell's Cheshire home was subjected to dawn raids by police and the former butler found himself accused of stealing 342 possessions from the woman he affectionately referred to as 'the boss', including various items of clothing, family photo albums and a £500,000 jewel-encrusted model boat given as a wedding present to Charles and Diana by the Emir of Bahrain.

Burrell protested his innocence, insisting that he had been asked to hold onto the items for safekeeping following Diana's death, but the British press and public savagely turned on the man for what they considered a shocking violation of the memory of the 'People's Princess'.

Diana had long referred to Burrell as 'my rock'; he travelled with her around the world and provided a much-needed shoulder to cry on

Paul Burrell's perceived betrayal of his former employer Princess Diana made him one of Britain's most unpopular men

The biggest shock, however, was yet to come. The trial itself was postponed until October the following year so as not to interfere with the Queen's Golden Jubilee celebrations, but collapsed almost immediately, with the jury dismissed and

Burrell's book, A Royal Duty, *stopped short of revealing the great secret that many suspected Prince Charles was desperately trying to conceal*

which she did indeed agree to let Burrell hold onto the items in question.

An open and shut case, it would seem – or perhaps not. Burrell was already hard at work on a book about his time with Diana when his case came to court. Cynics believe that the Queen's sudden change of heart came under pressure from Charles, who was keen to maintain Burrell's silence on the alleged rape of a royal footman, George Smith, by one of the Prince of Wales' senior aides – an event believed to have taken place in the late 80s and of which Burrell was suspected to have proof in the form of a taped interview with Diana herself.

If that was indeed the case, then Charles got his way; the issue went unmentioned in Burrell's book *A Royal Duty*, published in 2003. That said, the book's cliff-hanger ending – in which Burrell refers to a shared secret between himself and Diana and the possibility of further revelations in a second book – suggests that there may be a few twists and turns yet to come.

the accused acquitted of all charges. The reason? The Queen claimed to have suddenly remembered a conversation in

Prince Harry

On January 13th, 2005, the world choked on its collective breakfast after seeing the cover of Britain's *Sun* newspaper, which boasted a picture of Prince Harry sporting Second World War military fatigues and a swastika armband – a drink in one hand and a cigarette in the other – beneath the headline 'Harry The Nazi'.

The previous Saturday, just weeks before International Holocaust Memorial Day, Harry had attended a 'Colonial and Native'-themed fancy dress party at a friend's house in Wiltshire in full Nazi regalia – a move that shocked Jewish groups the world over.

Clarence House was itself embarrassed enough to immediately issue a full apology on behalf of the prince, whom they had long been attempting to portray as a young athlete with a military mind and a social conscience to match his late mother's – the Harry who helped out at a local Red Cross centre in the wake of the 2004 Asian tsunami, for example, or who dug roads and planted crops as part of a charity drive in Southern Africa.

The media, however, was more interested in Harry the party prince: the Harry who in October 2002 admitted to smoking cannabis (news that led to doctored 'Harry Pothead and the Philosopher's Stoned' images circulating on the internet) and who could be seen regularly drinking and enjoying himself with friends his own age.

As a result, Harry has found himself face to face with hordes of flashing cameras almost every time he steps out of one of London's upmarket nightclubs – a situation that in October 2004 led to a fracas outside the notoriously upper-class nightspot Pangaea, in which one photographer was left with a cut lip. The snapper in question claimed to have been lashed out at by a drunken Prince Harry, although royal minders insisted the prince was simply pushing a camera out of his own face.

Harry's ill-advised Nazi costume shocked the world when it made the front page of the Sun *in 2005*

THE Sun

30p

Thursday, January 13, 2005   30p   www.thesun.co.uk

HOLS FROM £9.50

LAST CHANCE TO JOIN

TOKEN 5 INSIDE

8-PAGE PULLOUT & BOOKING FORM

HARRY THE NAZI

Prince's swastika outfit at party

EXCLUSIVE

By JAMIE PYATT and
DUNCAN LARCOMBE

PRINCE Harry stuns partygoers
by attending a pal's birthday
bash dressed as a Nazi soldier.

Harry, 20, wore the swastika
and desert uniform of Rommel's
hated German Afrika Korps to
the party in West Littleton, Wilts.

Last night he said: "I am very
sorry if I have caused any
offence. It was a poor choice of
costume and I apologise."

Full Story — Pages 4 & 5

© THE SUN

A Misguided Princess

Princess Beatrice's choice in men came under close scrutiny following her fling with Paolo Liuzzo, who was implicated in the manslaughter of an American student

Andrew and Fergie's eldest daughter, Princess Beatrice, caused a royal stir in 2005 when it emerged that her boyfriend, the then 24-year-old Paolo Liuzzo, had previously faced jail on manslaughter charges due to his involvement in a drunken brawl that left a fellow student dead in 2002. Liuzzo avoided prison by pleading guilty to the lesser charge of assault and battery, but was dragged back to court in early 2006 after breaking his probation on a ski trip to Switzerland with Beatrice and her family. The 18-year-old subsequently ended the relationship at her mother's insistence, although rumours of an ongoing romance continued to circulate.

Prince Andrew was pulled over by police after his car was recorded travelling at around 60mph in a 40mph zone

In July 2002, Prince Andrew was pulled over by police after his car was recorded travelling at around 60mph in a 40mph zone just outside Heathrow Airport. Andrew explained that he had been speeding to catch a plane waiting to take him to Edinburgh for the final round of the British Open golf tournament and the officer chose to let the prince off with a verbal warning – a decision that prompted a chorus of voices railing against royal favouritism. Those same voices redoubled in strength later that year, when Princess Anne was let off with a verbal slap on the wrist and a £500 fine after her English bull terrier Dotty nipped and scratched two children in Windsor Great Park – an incident that would ordinarily have led to fines of up to £5,000 and a virtual guarantee of the animal being put down.

In early 1986, Diana and Fergie made the papers by strolling into upmarket London members' club Annabel's and knocking back champagne to celebrate the latter's impending marriage to Prince Andrew – all well and good, except that the pair were dressed as police officers. The controversy that followed concerned not only how the women had managed to circumnavigate Annabel's notoriously formal dress code, but whether or not they'd broken the law by 'impersonating' policewomen. Mercifully, such speculation was short-lived and the incident is now regarded as being among the finest examples of royal protocol being thrown to the wind in the name of good, honest fun.

Diana and Fergie became firm friends and shared a love of childish humour – as their decision to attend an upmarket London club dressed as police officers went to prove

Princess Anne's daughter Zara Philips quickly became known within the British press as the 'Royal Rebel' – a nod to her occasionally outlandish behaviour and party-oriented lifestyle. At 16, Zara shocked the establishment by having both her tongue and belly button pierced and was thereafter variously snapped sunbathing topless, falling out of nightclubs with

Equestrian Games in Germany and was subsequently awarded the BBC's Sports Personality of the Year – an honour previously received by her mother in 1971 for her own horse-riding exploits.

In 2003, a teacher previously fired from Eton College claimed to have done the lion's share of Prince Harry's art coursework in a bid to ensure Harry achieved the grades needed to guarantee his place at Sandhurst Royal Military Academy. Sarah Forsyth had even gone so far as to secretly tape a conversation with the prince as proof of her accusations. A British court agreed that she had been bullied out of her position at the school, but rejected her claims regarding the young prince and rebuked her illicit (not to mention illegal) recording of their conversation. Nor did the case affect Harry's military career: he subsequently entered Sandhurst following a gap year and graduated as a commissioned officer in April 2006.

a string of boyfriends and engaging in such seemingly unladylike activities as bungee jumping. Speculation that she was on the verge of being blacklisted from the Royal Family was, however, misguided: in 2006, Zara confounded her critics by winning a gold medal at the World

PART FIVE

ROYALS IN THE FIRING LINE

Royals throughout history have met with more than their fair share of untimely ends. A low life expectancy was simply part and parcel of being a ruler of early England, a job that came with enemies as standard and in which defending your kingdom meant standing knee-deep in bodies on the battlefield with the rest of your men.

On top of that there was the possibility of being killed in a hunting accident (William Rufus), murdered by a disgruntled mob (Edward II) or assassinated by an over-enthusiastic successor (Edward V), not to mention the danger of being often on horseback (Sweyn 'Forkbeard', William the Conqueror and William III all died after falling from their steeds).

In this chapter we'll be examining some of the historical meetings between the Royal Family and the grim spectre of death – some of them mere brushes, others head-on collisions: Edward the Martyr was murdered by his own stepmother, while Harold's fabled 'arrow in the eye' may not be all that it seems. There is also an account of the disastrous 'Nine Days Queen' and the infamous Babington Plot that conspired to end the life of Elizabeth I.

We will also be looking at the Gunpowder Plot that came within a hair's breadth of blowing up Parliament in November 1605, the public regicide that divided a nation in 1649 and various failed attempts upon the lives of George III, Queen Victoria and Edward VIII. Finally, there is an account of the tragic assassination in 1979 of Earl Mountbatten, Prince Philip's uncle – proof that life as a member of the Royal Family may now be significantly safer than in years gone by, and that dealing with dangerous adversaries still comes with the territory.

Edward the Martyr was murdered by his own stepmother, while Harold's fabled 'arrow in the eye' story may not be all that it seems

William Rufus, killed – possibly murdered – during a hunting trip in the New Forest. The 'Rufus Stone' marks the spot to this day

125

EDWARD II, THE MARTYR
(975–978)

Among Edward's many enemies was his own stepmother Elfrida, who felt that he had cheated her son Ethelred of the throne. On March 18th, 978, Edward interrupted a hunting trip in Wareham, Dorset, to drop in on Ethelred – just ten at the time – at nearby Corfe Castle. Elfrida offered him a glass of mead as he entered the gates on horseback, but as he raised it to his lips he was stabbed in the back by one of her attendants.

This so spooked his steed that it dragged him, one foot still in the saddle, all the way back down the hill to a stream, which was later said to have imparted healing properties as a result.

This was the first of many miracles associated with Edward's martyrdom: Queen Elfrida initially ordered the body hidden in a small wooden hut, with the result that a blind woman living therein found her sight completely restored; afterwards, the corpse was buried in a marsh near Wareham, but locals reputedly discovered it by means of an ethereal pillar of fire that hovered over the place of its interment.

In the 16th century, the relics were removed from Shaftsbury Abbey and hidden to protect them from desecration during the anti-monastic reign of Henry VIII; in 1931, they were rediscovered and 40 years later subjected to stringent tests that proved that the dead king had indeed been stabbed in the back and dragged along the ground by his horse.

That part of the legend, at least, appears to be true.

Edward's corpse took on miraculous properties following his martyrdom and rumours of its powers became the stuff of legend

The Bayeux Tapestry may hold the key to King Harold's much-debated cause of death

HAROLD II (Jan–Oct 1066)

Very little in English history has been mythologized quite like King Harold's infamous 'arrow in the eye' at the Battle of Hastings in 1066. The warrior king had more or less taken the upper hand in the fight when his forces fell for a feigned retreat by the Normans, thereafter being routed, pinned down and picked off one by one.

The 230ft (70m) Bayeux Tapestry has long been held to accurately describe the nature of the English king's passing in the section entitled 'Harold interfectus est' ('Harold is killed'), which shows a man, below the name 'Harold', grappling with what appears to be an arrow in the eye. However, closer examination of a soldier

being hacked apart to the right (beneath the words 'interfectus est') reveals a series of stitches beside his head that may once have shown another arrow, since lost. This would imply a more animated sequence of events in which Harold is first shot in the eye with an arrow and then, after falling to the ground, finished off by a Norman on horseback.

This would certainly corroborate the account offered by the chronicler Henry of Huntingdon, who describes how 'a shower of arrows fell around the king and he himself was pierced in the eye. A crowd of horsemen now burst in and the king, already wounded, was slain.' Either way, a pleasant end it most certainly was not.

LADY JANE GREY
(July 1553)

Few characters in history endured so raw a royal deal as the 'Nine Days Queen', who had the crown almost literally thrust upon her as part of a plot by her father-in-law, John Dudley, the Duke of Northumberland, who hoped to install his own son on the throne as a result.

Following the death of the short-lived Edward VI in July 1553, Dudley bullied Parliament into accepting the worldly and well-educated Jane as queen on account of her being Henry VII's granddaughter – a tenuous link, but one that they agreed to on the grounds that the legitimate heir, Edward's sister Mary, was a Catholic.

Jane was told of her accession and she attempted to reject the crown. Dudley refused to hear her complaints and the

On the February 12th, 1554, Jane was blindfolded and beheaded privately inside the Tower

following morning she was marched to the Tower of London, where the state apartments had been furnished to receive her.

The streets of London, however, were unusually silent: many people felt Mary – Catholic or otherwise – had been cheated of her rightful place on the throne. Jane understood this only too well and spent her short tenure in the Tower pleading with the Northumberlands to let her return the crown to its rightful owner – pleas that fell on deaf ears.

Mary, meanwhile, had amassed an army and was marching on London. The closer she came, the more Jane's council began to betray her until on July 19th – the ninth and final day of the young queen's rule – Mary was crowned in London's Cheapside and the streets rang with celebration.

Jane spent her few remaining days in the Tower: she was a prisoner of sorts, but when Mary enlisted a Catholic priest to convert her, it seemed as

Lady Jane Grey, whose tenure as the 'Nine Days Queen' is among the most tragic episodes in English history. Here she is depicted being led to the block for her execution

though her life might be spared. Such hopes were dashed, however, when Mary's marriage to Catholic Prince Philip of Spain set off a spate of Protestant revolts across the country, with many calling for Jane's restoration to the throne.

On the February 12th, 1554, Jane was blindfolded and beheaded privately inside the Tower – a luxury usually afforded only to royalty, and thus a mark of Queen Mary's remorse for having to kill the most ill-fated of monarchs.

ELIZABETH I
(1558–1603)

The Babington Plot to assassinate Queen Elizabeth I and return England to Catholicism under Mary Queen of Scots is one of the most dramatic episodes in the nation's history – a tangled web of coded letters, double crossings and regicidal intrigue.

The plot is named after one Anthony Babington, a Derbyshire nobleman who had rallied Catholics from across the country and even secured the support of an invasion force from King Philip of Spain in the event of a successful assassination. Mary herself was in captivity in Chartley Hall in Staffordshire at the time, but Babington kept her

Mary Queen of Scots was executed for her attempts to re-establish a Catholic claim to the throne

informed via coded letters smuggled into and out of the building in the hollow stoppers of barrels belonging to a local brewery.

The first letter was passed to Mary by a Catholic priest, Gilbert Gifford, in June 1586; she in turn penned a reply, in which she instructed Babington to contact her supporters in Paris. What

Babington didn't know was that Gifford was actually a double agent working for the secretary of state, Sir Francis Walsingham, who was transcribing every one of the coded letters en route and then having them unscrambled at his private cipher school.

When one of Babington's correspondences explicitly mentioned both the assassination of Elizabeth and the Spanish invasion force, Walsingham had all the evidence he needed. He stepped in and arrested the main conspirators on the August 15th, 1586, after which they were publicly executed at two separate ceremonies: Babington was among those hung, drawn and quartered at the first; so grim a spectacle that Elizabeth personally asked for the second group of traitors to be, more humanely, hung until they were dead.

Nor was Mary's eventual end any less unpleasant. Her beheading, at Fotheringhay Castle on February 8th of the following year, was badly mishandled: the first blow missed and shattered the back of her skull; the second only served to sever a main artery, spraying blood everywhere (including over one of her dogs, which reputedly later died of shock); even the third blow, although mercifully fatal, was poorly aimed, requiring the embarrassed executioner to even off the rough edges by using the blade of his axe like a saw.

JAMES I
(1603–1625)

Few of those who annually celebrate Guy
Fawkes Night know the real story behind
the tradition.

The Gunpowder Plot of 1605 coincided
with an end of Catholic patience for
James I, on whom many members of the
religious minority had pinned high hopes,
but who had ended up bowing to Puritan
pressure, reinstating recusancy fines for
those unwilling to renounce their faith and
having Catholic priests outlawed across
the land.

A man named Robert Catesby decided to
take action. On May 20th, 1604, Catesby
gathered together a group of trusted
Catholics in the Duck and Drake pub on
the Strand in London and there divulged to
them the details of his dangerous plan.

By March the following year, the group had
begun renting a cellar directly beneath the
Houses of Parliament and it was here that
they started storing up barrels of gunpowder
for the explosion due to coincide with the
forthcoming State Opening of Parliament –
an explosion that would, if all went to plan,
kill the king himself.

The job of lighting the fuse had been
given to Guy Fawkes, who would
subsequently make a break for the
continent and attempt to muster
international support for the coup.
Fawkes' co-conspirators, meanwhile,
would kidnap King James' first-born
daughter, Elizabeth, and install her on

King James I comes face
to face with his would-be
assassin, Guy Fawkes

entered the undercroft to light the fuse on November 4th, the authorities were there to arrest him.

Fawkes refused to name his co-conspirators until the king sanctioned torture of the worst kind by the interrogators, and eventually the plotters were rounded up and returned to London to be hung, drawn and quartered at one of the most grisly public spectacles in English history.

the throne as a puppet queen, thereafter forcing her to convert to Catholicism.

Unbeknown to them, however, word of their plans had already reached the government thanks to an anonymous tip-off from one conspirator with cold feet, with the result that, when Guy Fawkes

Guy Fawkes, however, still had one last trick up his sleeve, jumping off the executioner's scaffold at the last minute and breaking his neck in the process, thus saving himself the horror of being drawn and quartered while fully conscious.

CHARLES I
(1625–1649)

Charles incited the civil war that secured his downfall through a headstrong will that most took for stubbornness. His falling out with his policy makers created a rift so great that Charles had Parliament dissolved in 1629, thereafter ruling alone

The Roundhead leader Oliver Cromwell inspects the body of King Charles I, an action that reputedly led him to take pity on the executed monarch

for what became known as the 'Eleven Years Tyranny'.

National indignation led to an increasingly clear split between the Royalists (Cavaliers) and Parliamentarians (Roundheads), which in October 1642 blossomed into a full-scale civil war that eventually saw the king captured and tried for treason and 'other high crimes' in a specially commissioned court under the Roundhead leader Oliver Cromwell.

The king refused to plead at the trial, which began on January 2nd, 1649, and at the end of the month his death warrant was signed by the 59 separate judges of the tribunal.

Charles showed great dignity on the day of his execution, January 30th, 1649. It was a bitterly cold morning and the king reputedly wore two shirts to ensure that the crowd wouldn't see him shivering and think him afraid.

Some maintain that the Hangman of London, Richard Brandon, refused any part in the affair and that a substitute had to be called up from Ireland. Either way, it was a short ceremony: Charles' head was

> *Cromwell tried to set the nation at ease by having Charles' head sewn back onto his body so that his family could pay their last respects, but it was too late*

held aloft, as tradition demanded, but the usual declaration ('Behold, the head of a traitor') was passed on, out of respect.

Public remorse over the affair was almost immediate. Cromwell tried to set the nation at ease by having Charles' head sewn back onto his body so that his family could pay their last respects, but it was too late: that night, a radical anti-monarchist was rumoured to have had his eyes pecked out by crows; a falling star was seen blazing above Whitehall; and handkerchiefs dipped in the late monarch's blood were already said to be displaying miraculous properties. The cult of the martyr king had begun.

GEORGE III (1760–1820)

The increasingly insane English monarch found himself the target of similarly unhinged assailants on more than one occasion. In 1786, a disturbed London lady called Margaret Nicholson attempted to stab the king outside St James's Palace; the woman was immediately set upon and dragged away screaming by royal aides while the unharmed king looked on with concern. 'Pray do not harm the poor woman,' he is said to have called after them, a sign, perhaps, that he

King George III was on more than one occasion forced to contend with potential assassination

sympathized with the mentally unbalanced even when they endangered his life.

A potentially more serious incident occurred on May 15th, 1800, when the king was attending an evening performance at the Theatre Royal in London's Drury Lane. Seated in the stalls, unbeknown to the king, was an ex-soldier named James Hadfield, who had been severely delusional since being struck on the head eight times with a sabre in battle. Hadfield had also become involved with a movement of millennialists obsessed with the Second Coming of Christ – an event that he personally believed would be brought about by his own execution for regicide.

As a result, during the customary singing of the English National Anthem, Hadfield stood up and fired a pistol into the Royal Box, missing the king completely, and afterwards shouted: 'God bless your Royal Highness, I like you very well. You are a good fellow.' Execution, however, eluded him: Hadfield's lawyer got him off on an insanity plea and the failed assassin spent the rest of his life in a mental hospital. Once again, the king may well have empathized entirely.

VICTORIA (1837–1901)

Psychologists have written extensively on the complexes that caused so many young Englishmen to give up their freedom for a moment of infamy, firing pocket pistols harmlessly packed with powder, paper or tobacco in the direction of Her Majesty, including John William Bean (1842), William Hamilton (1849) and 17-year-old Arthur O'Connor (1872).

Sentences for such crimes ranged from a year's imprisonment and twenty lashes to transportation to a Commonwealth penal colony, although the latter was reserved for more serious offenders, such as Robert Pate, who in 1850 struck Victoria on the head with his cane.

Arguably Victoria's luckiest escape, however, was her last. In 1882, as the Queen was disembarking from a train at

In 1850, Robert Pate was arrested after striking Queen Victoria on the head with his cane

Victoria regularly found herself fired at by pistols containing nothing more harmful than paper

Windsor Station, a youth named Roderick MacLean fired a loaded pistol at the queen from a range of just a few feet – reputedly in response to her having ignored the poems that he regularly posted to her. As chance would have it, an Eton student managed to deflect the boy's arm with his umbrella just before the gun went off, causing the bullet to miss Victoria. MacLean was subsequently spared the death penalty after being deemed insane.

EDWARD VIII (Jan–Dec 1936)

On July 16th, 1936, Edward took part in the traditional military procession of Trooping the Colour in Hyde Park. Around 12.30pm, the parade began filtering through Wellington Arch.

It was at this point that a man in the crowd dropped the newspaper that he had been clutching tightly, to reveal a pistol, which he then aimed at the monarch. A skirmish with police ensued, in which the gun was hurled into the road.

King Edward VIII's well-documented sympathy for Adolf Hitler may well have made him a prime target for assassination by radical Austrian communists

The would-be assassin – whose real name turned out to be Jerome Brannigan – claimed that the 'assassination' was actually part of a sting by MI5. He said that he'd contacted the intelligence agency after being approached by members of a 'foreign power', who had promised him £150 in return for assassinating the king. According to his story, he'd only been going through the motions at the event so as not to raise suspicions, but MI5 had deserted him at the last minute.

His claim was thrown out of court at the time, but now seems to contain more than an element of truth. The Metropolitan Police later confirmed that MI5 had indeed been in touch with Brannigan prior to the event, while a

It was at this point that a man in the crowd dropped the newspaper that he had been clutching tightly, to reveal a pistol

scribble on the back of the newspaper that he dropped at the scene – 'May I love you' – is now believed to have been a message to his housemate May Galley, close friend to a group of Austrian activists who were later linked with the Austrian communist party.

Was this the 'foreign power' of which Brannigan spoke? If so, it is possible that the Austrian communists were hoping to rid Europe of a king increasingly enamoured of the German Führer. As if to prove it, the young king had received a telegram, that same afternoon, from none other than Hitler himself. 'I have just received the news of the abominable attempt on the life of Your Majesty,' it read, 'and send my heartiest congratulations on your escape.'

EARL MOUNTBATTEN
(died 1979)

Few events have shattered the perceived bubble of security surrounding the Royal Family like the assassination in 1979 of Earl Mountbatten of Burma, a noted navy admiral, greatly admired statesman and uncle of Prince Philip.

On August 27th, Mountbatten and his immediate family were holidaying in their summer home at Mullaghmore in the Republic of Ireland – an area they had been visiting regularly for many years and where they were much liked by the local community.

Around mid-morning, the family left their majestic home at Classiebawn Castle for a day's fishing out of Donegal Bay on their private 30ft (9m) boat, Shadow V. No sooner had they left the harbour, however, than the vessel was lifted into the air and blown into a constellation of wooden shards by a powerful bomb – the work, it later transpired, of the Provisional IRA, which emphasized its anti-royalist sentiments by killing 18 British soldiers in County Down on the same day.

Of those in the boat, Earl Mountbatten, his 14-year-old grandson, Nicholas, and a 15-year-old local boy working as a crew member were killed outright; his daughter's mother-in-law died later in hospital. The IRA member Thomas McMahon was sentenced to life in prison a month later, but was released in 1998 under the Good Friday Agreement, a decision that horrified the Mountbatten family.

Earl Mountbatten, his 14-year-old grandson, Nicholas, and a 15-year-old local boy working as a crew member were killed outright

Earl Mountbatten's death in an IRA bomb-blast shocked the world – not least because he and his family had been soft targets, killed for their connections to the British Royal Family alone

PART SIX

DIANA'S LIFE AND DEATH

**Few events have shattered the collective heart
of a nation like the car crash that ended the life
of Diana, Princess of Wales, in 1997. The
subsequent outpouring of grief proved that she
remained, to use her own phrase, a 'queen of
people's hearts'.**

The accident may also have been one of
the most public tragedies of all time – the
number of related articles and opinions
circulating in the papers, on the airwaves
and on the internet is almost
unprecedented – but various questions
remain unanswered.

What happened to the mysterious white
Fiat Uno initially believed to have collided
with Diana's car? Why did all the CCTV
cameras in the tunnel stop working just
moments before the crash? And what
really went on in the back of the
ambulance that took Diana to the hospital?

All are questions that will be addressed in
this chapter, which also features a
chronology of events leading up to the
accident, an insight into the subsequent
public relations fiasco that almost ended
the British monarchy, a profile of the most
notable Diana memorials and a short
biography of the erstwhile princess herself.

*Princess Diana's
death has been
shrouded in
unanswered
questions and
accusations
of a cover-up*

Chronicle of a Death Retold

Arguably the darkest day in the history of the modern monarchy, August 31st, 1997 has been written into legend as the date the British public lost their 'People's Princess'. But what really happened in the small hours of that fateful morning in Paris?

The CCTV images of Dodi and Diana being briefed by Henri Paul before leaving the hotel are now legendary

SATURDAY, AUGUST 30TH

3.15pm

Dodi and Diana's ten-day Mediterranean cruise aboard the Fayed family yacht ends with a flight on a private Harrods plane to Paris, where the couple are met by 41-year-old Henri Paul, the Ritz security officer who will later drive them to their deaths. For now, however, he takes them to the Paris Ritz itself – owned by Dodi's father, Egyptian entrepreneur Mohamed Al Fayed – where the lovers are booked into the $2,000-per-night Imperial Suite. Hordes of paparazzi are already mustering at the doors when they arrive.

The Paris Ritz, owned by Dodi's father

9.00pm

The couple leave the hotel, fashionably late for their 8.30pm reservation at trendy bistro *Benoit*, but turn back at the last minute when it becomes obvious that the steadily massing paparazzi will make informal dining impossible to enjoy. Instead, they return to the more fortified Ritz, settling into the upmarket *L'Espadon* restaurant – although their casual bistro clothes (cowboy boots and jeans for Dodi, white slacks and a blazer for Diana) draw unwanted attention from countless gawping diners. Despairing, Dodi orders their meals to be sent upstairs so that the lovers can finish their dinner in the privacy of their suite.

11.30pm

Wined and dined and wanting to go out, Dodi settles on a ruse to escape the photographers outside the Ritz, engaging his regular driver to set off as a decoy in his black Range Rover – a car familiar to the paparazzi – while he and Diana slip unnoticed out the back door and depart in a blacked-out Mercedes S-Class on loan from the hotel.

SUNDAY, AUGUST 31ST

12.20am

A Ritz security camera inadvertently catches the now infamous final shot of Dodi and Diana standing by the back door as Henri Paul explains the details of their secret departure. The couple are laughing and joking when they finally slide into the car along with 29-year-old Trevor Rees-Jones, a personal Fayed security guard. Less than a minute later, their plan has been foiled by the paparazzi, who give chase en masse.

12.25am

The entourage proceeds as planned until it reaches the Place de la Concorde, where Henri Paul suddenly jumps a red light, picking up speed along the riverside and roaring into the Pont de l'Alma tunnel. It is here that Paul loses control of the vehicle, scraping into the right-hand wall before veering to the left and crashing into a concrete pillar, after which the car spins to a stop. Dodi and the driver are killed instantly; the former sprawled across the back seat, the latter thrown halfway through the windshield. Trevor Rees-Jones – the only person wearing a seatbelt – is concussed, his jaw shattered and his tongue severed in

the impact. Diana is unconscious but alive on the floor of the car.

12.27am

A French physician, Dr Frederic Mailliez, races back to the scene after passing the collision in his car. By the time he arrives, a number of paparazzi have opened the doors and are already busily snapping away. (One of these photographers, Christian Martinez, is later accused of telling police officers on the scene to get lost and let him do his job.)

12.30am

Mailliez attends to Diana – whom he doesn't recognize at this point – helping her up from the floor and into a position that won't obstruct her breathing. She is drifting in and out of consciousness, mumbling and gesturing wildly and letting out the occasional small cry. Mailliez notes that she is superficially unharmed save for a dislocated arm and a cut on her forehead, so he applies an oxygen mask from his car and tries to reassure her until the emergency services arrive. On all sides, the flashbulbs of photographers lend the grim air of a morbid awards ceremony.

SUNDAY, AUGUST 31ST CONTINUED

12.32am

The first ambulance arrives on the scene. As she is being removed from the car, Diana suffers what is later said to be a cardiac arrest, leading to the ambulance crew's controversial decision to intubate, ventilate and treat her in the back of the vehicle while still at the scene.

1.30am

Almost an hour later, the ambulance finally leaves for the hospital, escorted by police and with the roads ahead closed and cleared. Even so, the vehicle drives slowly for fear of aggravating Diana's internal injuries – so slowly (25mph) that she isn't delivered to the intensive care unit of the nearby Hospital la Pitié-Salpêtrière until after 2am.

The Sunday papers of August 31st worked right up to the wire to get the latest on Diana's condition, but only a few managed to go to press with the full, shocking story

*The Flame of Liberty, overlooking the Pont de l'Alma tunnel, became a temporary
focus point for tokens of public grief following the crash itself*

2.10am

Diana, now in the hands of the hospital
surgeons, goes into a massive cardiac
arrest. Subsequent administrations of
adrenalin, electric shocks and external
heart massages continue in vain for
almost two hours.

4.00am

Diana's death is officially recorded
by doctors.

5.30am

News of Diana's passing is conveyed to
the world via an impromptu press
conference. Her body remains on site until
2pm, at which point Prince Charles arrives
with Diana's sisters to retrieve it. By the
time it is ushered onto the private royal
jet, at 3.30pm, barely 24 hours have
passed since the former princess and her
beloved Dodi touched down in the most
romantic city on earth.

An Elusive Truth

Dodi's father, Mohamed Al Fayed, has been among the most vocal of conspiracy theorists, going so far as to offer a $20 million reward to anyone able to prove a royal cover-up

Few events in history have become the subject of feverish hypothesis quite like the car accident that ended the lives of Dodi and Diana. A huge amount of alternative theories is currently circulating, and shows no sign of abating despite the investigation by former UK police chief Lord Stevens, which found that there was no conspiracy.

Diana, the theorists claim, had simply become too wild a force for the notoriously starchy English establishment; her frank interviews with the media were painting the royals in an unfavourable light, while her glamorous lifestyle, romantic affairs and regular appearances in the tabloids were an embarrassment for Charles and his family.

Her attachment to Dodi Fayed – heir to his father's Harrods fortune and occasional movie producer – was rumoured to be the last straw. Some claim that the $205,400 diamond ring presented to her at their last dinner at the Ritz was a token of their engagement; others say that Diana was pregnant with his child, a fact that she apparently tried to impart to the ambulance crew by rubbing her belly, and which the Royal Family did their best to cover up by having her body embalmed before it left Paris.

Lord Stevens' report rejected such claims outright, but some insist that the possibility of the future King of England having a half-Arabic stepbrother was too much for Charles and Prince Philip, who plotted in conjunction with MI6 to have Dodi and Diana killed. Indeed, one of the secret service's former members, Richard Tomlinson, was arrested in 1997 after suggesting that MI6 had been tracking Diana for months, pointing to the presence of various agents in Paris at the time of the crash (including one posted in the Ritz itself) and noting similarities between Diana's accident and a planned MI6 assassination of the Serbian despot Slobodan Milosevic.

Diana, the theorists claim, had become too wild a force for the notoriously starchy English establishment

Conspiracy Theories

Regardless of the truth behind such claims, speculation surrounding Diana's death is unlikely to end anytime soon. Here we explore the elements of what conspiracy hunters would have you believe is one of the greatest cover-ups of the 20th century.

The chauffeur

The official line from French authorities was that samples of blood taken from Henri Paul at the scene showed him to have been dosed up on antidepressants and more than three times over the legal alcohol limit at the time of the crash. Such accusations were corroborated by anonymous sources at the Ritz, which claimed that Paul had a persistent drink problem and had been 'drunk as a pig' on the night in question.

Friends and neighbours, however, rushed to his defence, asserting that no one had seen him in a bar that evening and pointing to hotel CCTV footage that appeared to show Paul in full control as he spoke to Dodi and Diana before their departure. Dodi's father, Mohamed Al Fayed, has been among the driver's most impassioned defenders, insisting that his son would have fired Paul on the spot if he had appeared even vaguely intoxicated and asserting that the drink-driving accusation is simply part of a wider cover-up.

The white car

The fact that only Trevor Rees-Jones was wearing a seatbelt at the time of the collision has led many to believe that Paul's sudden acceleration into the tunnel was a spontaneous decision, rather than part of a grand plan, as has the fact that the tunnel actually offered a significantly longer route to their destination than the overland Avenue de Champs Elysees.

So why did Paul choose the tunnel? The obvious answer would be to lose the paparazzi (the Champs Elysees route is peppered with traffic lights), but several witnesses described seeing two cars and a motorbike forcing the doomed Mercedes into the tunnel by blocking the overland exit; others recall a white Fiat Uno that raced ahead of Diana's car into the tunnel –

evidence that corroborated a police statement (quickly retracted) that flecks of white paint had been found on the wreckage, and that the authorities were keen to speak to the owner of the mysterious car in question.

Regardless, the role played by these phantom vehicles is hard to establish for a single reason: the tunnel's 17 CCTV cameras mysteriously stopped working for an hour at midnight – a grim coincidence that conspiracy theorists would argue is anything but.

It didn't take long for the British newspapers to weigh into the debate surrounding Diana's death

The ambulance

Even those who balk at the various conspiracies surrounding the crash itself find it hard to justify the ambulance crew's decision to treat Diana there and then – a decision that has since been questioned by countless high-ranking doctors, all of whom stress that the obvious thing to do would have been to rush her to hospital for immediate treatment.

When the ambulance did finally leave the scene – more than an hour after the collision itself – it did so at a crawl speed of 25mph, taking over half an hour to travel no more than four miles. Not only that, but it ignored several intensive care units closer to the scene than the one at the Pitié-Salpêtrière – including those at the Val de Grace, the Hotel Dieu, Lariboisiere and the nearby private American Hospital.

Conspiracy theorists argue that the ambulance crew, in on the plot along with French police, finished Diana off on the journey. By the time the surgeons went to work on her, they say, she was just moments from death – which is in stark contrast to the initial diagnosis of Dr Frederic Mailliez, who deemed her condition 'not catastrophic'.

Unsettling signs: more fuel for the conspiracy fire

In 2003, a letter from Diana to her butler, Paul Burrell, was made public, in which she expressed fears that Prince Charles wanted her dead and was 'planning an accident in my car, brake failure and a serious head injury'.

Witnesses claimed to have seen a flash inside the tunnel moments before the collision, corroborating former MI6 agent Richard Tomlinson's accusations that a purpose-built light – possibly carried by the mysterious white Fiat – had been used to blind Diana's driver.

Why wasn't Diana, reputedly a strong advocate of seatbelt use, strapped in? Some claim that the car had been swapped at the last minute for a model in which certain seatbelts had been deliberately tampered with, rendering them unfit for use.

CCTV cameras in the tunnel reputedly stopped working just moments before the crash

Within two and a half hours of Diana's removal from the site, the tunnel was cleared, disinfected and re-opened to traffic, thus removing the possibility of retrieving potentially important evidence.

The Royal Family's somewhat unusual request that Diana's body be embalmed that same morning meant that any post-mortem following her return to England would have great difficulty in ascertaining the true nature of her assing – or possible pregnancy.

An Unfortunate Reaction

No one was expecting a prolonged period of public mourning by the royals, holidaying in the Scottish retreat of Balmoral when the news broke.

Diana had been stripped of her magisterial titles following her divorce in 1996, while a string of tabloid-friendly affairs – including those with England rugby captain Will Carling, army officer James Hewitt and Canadian pop star Bryan Adams – had seen her more or less excommunicated from the Royal Family.

So profound is the public affection for Diana that floral tributes are still left outside Kensington Palace on the anniversary of her death. Those shown here mark eight years since the accident

The fact that the royals refused to appear in public in the days following the crash, however, let alone make any kind of public statement on the matter, enraged a grief-stricken nation. After all, this was a time when people were sleeping on the streets of central London just so they could be near Diana's body, lying in state at her former home of Kensington Palace; a time when her wrought-iron gates faced onto a sea of tens of thousands of bouquets, and when mile-long queues of people waited patiently to sign her various condolence books.

As the week wore on, the lack of a flag at half-mast above Buckingham Palace became seen as a symbol of royal disregard for Diana's death (even though tradition dictated that the only flag on display there should be the Royal Standard, which never flies at half-mast). The British front-page headlines said it all: 'Your People Are Suffering: Speak To Us

A flag now flies above Buckingham Palace, a royal concession to the nation's grief

Ma'am', read *The Mirror*; 'Where Is Our Queen? Where Is Her Flag?' screamed *The Sun*.

> *One in every four Britons felt the monarchy should be abolished*

Around the same time, a major survey revealed that one in every four Britons felt the monarchy had become irrelevant and should be abolished. The Queen was plunged into a crisis the likes of which she had never known.

A warming of the cold front

Finally, on Thursday, September 4th – two days before Diana's funeral – royal obstinacy gave way. The Queen and her family appeared in public following an evening service in Balmoral, pausing to inspect some of the floral tributes laid outside the church and speaking to members of the crowd. The following day, they returned to Buckingham Palace, where the Queen made arguably the most difficult speech of her life.

In the address, broadcast live from the Chinese Dining Room, Elizabeth II attempted to redress the balance by referring to Diana as 'an exceptional and gifted human being,' whom she 'admired and respected', and who 'never lost her capacity to smile and laugh, nor to inspire others with her warmth and kindness'. Around the same time, the order was given to the Queen's Flag Sergeant to raise the Union Jack at half-mast during the funeral, an unprecedented break with tradition that showed just how desperate the situation had become.

The following morning, over a million people lined the streets of London in dutiful reverence as Diana's coffin wound its way silently from Kensington Palace to Westminster Abbey (more than 2.5 billion are believed to have watched the procession on television); even the Queen dutifully bowed her head as it passed. The ceremony itself, meanwhile, was studded with celebrities (Tom Hanks, Nicole Kidman and Steven Spielberg, among others), and saw speeches from Diana's sisters and a tribute performance of the reworked *Candle In The Wind* by Elton John.

It was the eulogy given by her brother, however, that caused the most controversy, with its barely veiled criticism

158

As Diana's funeral cortege passed through London, Charles later reported, you 'could hear a pin drop'. Here he is pictured with his father, sons and erstwhile brother-in-law, Earl Spencer

of the monarchy that had hung his sister out to dry. Diana, he said, had been 'someone with a natural nobility who was classless and who proved in the last year that she needed no royal title to continue to generate her particular brand of magic.'

The speech, broadcast on loudspeakers outside the abbey, ended with so riotous an ovation from the assembled masses that the sound of applause swept into the building itself. If the royals heard it, however, their faces betrayed nothing.

Princess Diana: A Life in Short

Despite being educated at highly respected private schools first in Norfolk and then Kent, Lady Diana Spencer failed her O Levels and was regarded as an under-achiever academically, although she was a talented singer and ballerina.

...les in 1977, during a ...iss finishing school (he ...ttached to her sister, ... time), but it wasn't until three years later that the prince was urged to make a more formal commitment to Diana – reputedly at the insistence of his former girlfriend (and future wife), Camilla Parker-Bowles.

Their engagement was announced on February 24th, 1981, with the wedding taking place at St Paul's Cathedral on July 29th – an event boasting over 3,500

The newly weds finally dispensed with royal protocol on the balcony of Buckingham Palace and gave the public – and the press – the kiss they had been waiting for

invited guests, drawing more than a billion television viewers and sealed with a kiss that made the front pages of newspapers around the world.

Overnight, Diana had become Her Royal Highness the Princess of Wales, Britain's future queen and the third most important woman in the country after Elizabeth II and her mother. With the birth of her two sons, William (b1982) and Harry (b1984), it seemed as though all the pieces of the dynastic jigsaw had fallen into place.

Charles and Diana's wedding was a spectacular event boasting over 3,500 invited guests, drawing more than a billion television viewers and sealed with a kiss that made the front pages of newspapers around the world

Happiness, however, proved more elusive
and behind the public facade lay a
princess in crisis, with bouts of post-natal
depression and recurring episodes of
bulimia – aggravated by the stifling
formality of royal life – that reputedly led
to several suicide attempts. By the mid-
80s, her marriage was in crisis: the royals
blamed Diana's unconventional
waywardness; Diana blamed her
husband's ongoing infatuation with his
childhood sweetheart, Camilla. Whatever
the cause, the couple were separated on
December 9th, 1992, with their divorce
finalized on August 28th, 1996.

Despite losing her title, Diana continued to
use her high profile to champion various
charitable causes, most notably alleviating
the ravages of AIDS (in 1987 she was
seen holding the hand of an AIDS sufferer
at a time when many still believed the
disease could be transmitted by mere
physical contact) and campaigning against
landmines. That same public profile was
also her undoing, however, leading as it
did to the constant hounding of her
romantic life by the paparazzi and, as a
result, to her untimely death in 1997.

Diana was laid to rest on her family's

estate at Althorp, buried on a small island
at the centre of an ornamental lake, home
to four black swans representing

guardians of the afterlife. The path leading
to the lake is lined with 36 oak trees – one
for every year of her short life.

*Charles' second marriage had none of the
worldwide attention lavished on his wedding to
Diana – but after so much negative publicity, the
couple seemed grateful for a degree of privacy*

A Princess Preserved

From the ocean of flowers blocking the gates to Kensington Palace in the days following the accident to the various, more permanent memorials erected in Diana's memory, tributes to the People's Princess have come in many forms.

Diana Memorial Fountain, Hyde Park, London

Mired in controversy, the most official of Diana memorials was closed due to problems with flooding a day after its grand opening by the Queen in July 2004 (a ceremony that saw the Spencers and the Windsors united for the first time since the funeral). Costing £3.6 million to build and £250,000 a year to maintain, US architect Kathryn Gustafson's enormous oval ring of running water has attracted more than its fair share of critics, including Mohamed Al Fayed, who referred to it as 'a sewer'.

Flame of Liberty, Paris

Not an official memorial, but this full-size, gold-leaf-covered reproduction of the torch carried by New York's Statue of Liberty sits on top of the entrance to the Pont de l'Alma tunnel in which Diana and Dodi lost their lives, and as such became a repository for countless tributes and messages from well-wishers in the years following the accident.

Diana and Dodi Memorial, Harrods, London

At the base of the central Egyptian escalator on the lower ground floor of Mohamed Al Fayed's mammoth shopping emporium stands a permanent tribute to

Mohamed Al Fayed's tribute to the dead couple draws scores of eager tourists on a daily basis

the late couple, featuring portraits of the pair linked by a gilded frame in the shape of two Ds, plus a pyramid encasing both the wine glass Diana used in the Paris Ritz on the night of her death and the ring – believed to be an engagement ring – given to her by Dodi at the same dinner.

Candle In The Wind 1997, by Elton John

A reworking of John's 1973 tribute to the actress Marilyn Monroe, with the lyrics altered to suit their new subject (the opening line 'Goodbye Norma Jean' became 'Goodbye England's Rose'). It was performed in public for the first and only time at Diana's funeral, although that didn't stop it becoming the second best-selling single of all time (after Bing Crosby's *White Christmas*), shifting 33 million units across the world and with the proceeds used to establish the Diana, Princess of Wales Memorial Fund.

Elton John has only ever performed his reworked Candle In The Wind once – at Diana's funeral

871–899: Alfred The Great

The only English king to be remembered as 'the Great' earned his title by arresting the advance of marauding Vikings through the country. A keen warrior, Alfred is reputed in legend to have disguised himself as a minstrel and entered the camp of his Danish enemy Guthram in a daring reconnaissance mission before the infamous Battle of Edington (878).

939–946: Edmund I, The Magnificent

Fatally stabbed at a celebratory banquet in the village of Pucklechurch after spotting

and engaging with an exiled thief named Liofa in the crowd. Liofa was himself killed in the fracas.

975–978: St Edward II, The Martyr

Edward made many enemies during his short reign, among them his own stepmother, Elfrida, who had him stabbed in the back during a visit to her home in Corfe Castle.

Alfred, in disguise, taking refuge in the house of an old peasant woman and famously burning her cakes

1013–1014: Sweyn 'Forkbeard'

The Viking ruler Sweyn succeeded in driving out the ill-counselled English King Ethelred the Unready and taking the crown for himself, although he died just weeks after his coronation, following a fall from his horse.

1016–1035: Canute

Canute's frustration at the endless flattery of his obsequious courtiers came to a head when he overheard one gushing about how the king could control even the oceanic tides. To demonstrate the limits of royal power, Canute led his men to the water's edge in the coastal village of Bosham, West Sussex, and there commanded the waves to go back, delighting in their surprise when the sea rolled on regardless.

1035–1042: Harthacanute

Invaded England with a large fleet to claim the crown from his dead brother, Harold Harefoot, whose body he had thrown into a marsh. Harthacanute became extremely unpopular with the English following heavy increases in national taxation. In 1041, the people of Worcester killed two of the king's tax collectors in protest; Harthacanute, in reply, had the entire city sacked and burned.

Canute proving his inability to influence the tides

1066: Harold II

Childless until the end of his reign, Edward the Confessor's deathbed wish that Harold Godwinson succeed him was disputed by many – among them William, Duke of Normandy. The newly crowned Harold had only just defeated another claimant (Norway's Harold Hardrada, at the Battle of Stamford Bridge in Northumbria) when William's ships laid anchor in Pevensey, Sussex. Harold marched his men south at an incredible pace, meeting William's army at a field in Hastings and engaging them in a gruelling battle that the English eventually lost after falling for a 'feigned flight' tactic by the Norman forces. Harold died in battle, although exactly how remains a subject of much debate among historians.

Harold's men were battle-weary and broken-spirited by the time they met William's at Hastings – but were it not for the Norman tactics, they might have prevailed regardless

1066–1087:
William The Conqueror

During the reign of Edward the Confessor there was just one stone castle in the whole of England; by the time William the Conqueror died in 1087 – after a falling beam struck his horse and threw him against the pommel of his saddle – there were 27. Nor was it just through architectural expansion that the Norman king consolidated his power: his ruthless suppression of revolts across the country is legendary, with the infamous Harrying of the North (1069–70) killing up to 150,000. Perhaps most notable, however, was the commissioning of the Domesday Survey in 1085, the result of which was a book, extant to this day, detailing the financial value of every piece of land in the kingdom, thus offering an unprecedented base for national taxation.

William's wide-ranging reforms changed the face of England

1087–1100: William II, Rufus

Named Rufus due to his red hair and ruddy complexion, William the Conqueror's favourite son was far from popular among his own people, or even within his own court. He died after being pierced through the heart by an arrow while hunting in the New Forest; the bowman, Walter Tyrel, said it was an accident, although many suspected an assassination orchestrated by William's brother Henry, who afterwards claimed the throne for his own.

Henry I may have had his brother killed in order to cement his claim to the throne

1100–1132: Henry I

Henry's reign was blighted when the White Ship carrying his two sons hit a rock in the English Channel and sank, killing all on board bar a butcher from Rouen. Grief-stricken, Henry put it in writing that his daughter, Matilda, would become queen, but this was ignored by Stephen of Blois, who raced across the Channel following Henry's death in 1135 and seized the crown for himself. A period of civil war followed, with the result that Henry, son of Matilda and Geoffrey of Anjou, was made royal heir, giving rise to a line of kings known variously as the Angevins (from Anjou) or Plantagenets (from the sprig of *planta genista* blossom that Geoffrey was famous for wearing in his hat).

1154–1189: Henry II

Henry raised his friend Thomas Becket to the position of Archbishop of Canterbury in an effort to fuse church and state, but Becket infuriated his liege by becoming a dedicated champion of the former. According to legend, a band of loyal knights in 1170 overheard Henry, at his wit's end, crying: 'Will no one rid me of this turbulent priest?' The knights then travelled to Canterbury, where they murdered Thomas as he prayed at the altar of his cathedral, lopping off the crown of his head and scattering his brains over the stone floor. Becket was canonized by Pope Alexander barely three years after his death and the site of the grisly murder became a hallowed place of pilgrimage.

Thomas Becket's grisly murder in Canterbury Cathedral

1189–1199: Richard I, The Lionheart

Crusading warrior king Richard personally barred Jews from his coronation ceremony, which led to rumours that he had ordered a massacre and resulted in many of London's Jews being beaten to death and burnt alive. Despite ruling for ten years, Richard – believed by many to have been a homosexual – spent a total of just ten months in England, and never tried to hide his loathing for the country.

1199–1216: John

King John was hugely unpopular with his own people, as well as politically tactless (he had to be recalled from Ireland after mocking the customs of Irish princes) and possibly stupid (he managed to lose the crown jewels when his convoy was caught out by the tide while crossing the Wash estuary in East Anglia). Civil war resulted in John being forced to sign the Magna Carta of 1215, an important document which limited the powers of English kings by forcing them to follow legal procedure in punishing subjects.

Richard the Lionheart, epitome of the crusading warrior king

1216–1272: Henry III

Crowned aged nine with his mother's toque in the absence of the crown lost by his father, Henry grew up to be obsessed with Edward the Confessor, going so far as to initiate the rebuilding of Westminster Abbey in his honour and having himself buried in the saint's original coffin after moving the kingly relics to a more resplendent tomb.

1272–1307: Edward I

With the majority of foreign lands having been lost by politically inept predecessors, Edward, known as the 'Hammer of the Scots', decided to consolidate power at home, first by ending Welsh independence and then by embarking on a drawn-out and disastrous war against Scotland. The latter led to the Battle of Falkirk in 1298, in which up to 15,000 Scots lost their lives; seven years later, the Scottish leader and popular hero William Wallace was captured and tried as 'king of the outlaws', thereafter being hung, drawn and quartered in London's Smithfield and his head stuck upon a pike on London Bridge.

William Wallace, the Scottish rebel, was tortured mercilessly before his execution under Edward I

1307–1327: Edward II

Repulsed his own court by appearing to take a male lover, Piers Gaveston, who was murdered by his enemies in 1312. Edward then turned his affections to the Despensers, a father and son team that reputedly plotted against Edward's wife Isabella; the queen subsequently removed herself to France before returning with a lover of her own, Roger Mortimer, and leading a rebellion that saw the Despensers executed and the king forced to abdicate. Edward was later murdered by having a red-hot iron forced into his anus, then believed to be a just end for homosexuals.

Despite being famous for his court cookery book, Richard II died in prison of suspected self-starvation

1377–1399: Richard II

Richard's court produced a cookery book, *The Forme of Cury*, outlining the preparation of such royal delights as Crustardes of Fyssh, Mylates of Pork and Lesshes Fryed in Lentoun. Forced into abdication in 1399, he died a prisoner in Pontefract Castle the following year.

1399–1413: Henry IV

Suffered from a debilitating skin condition, rumoured by his contemporaries to be leprosy, although now believed to have been a severe form of eczema. Early in his career it was prophesied that Henry would die in Jerusalem: this was widely believed to mean that he would perish on a holy crusade, although he eventually succumbed to a fit and died in the Jerusalem Chamber of Westminster Abbey in 1413.

1413–1422: Henry V

Shakespeare's favourite warrior king achieved a spectacular victory against a much larger French force at Agincourt in 1415, after which he marched to Paris and forced the signing of the Treaty of Troyes (1420), effectively cementing his position as the future French king – although his death from dysentery, two years later, meant that his grand plans never came to fruition.

Henry V leading his troops on a stunningly successful military campaign to capture the French throne in the name of England

1422–1471: Henry VI

Crowned while still a baby – and presiding over his first parliamentary meetings from his mother's arms – Henry VI turned out to be among the most incapable of English rulers, and a stark contrast to his formidable father. His inherent weakness led to a pitched battle for dynastic succession, known as the War of the Roses, between two royal houses: the Red Rose of Lancaster (of which Henry was an ineffectual leader) and the White Rose of York. Henry was deposed in 1461 before being briefly restored to the throne (1470) and then finally stabbed to death in the Tower (1471).

1483–1485: Richard III

Richard has been written into history as the murderer of his nephews, 12-year-old King Edward and his younger brother, in the Tower. That said, the dark side of his reputation owes much to negative Tudor propaganda, not to mention an unfavourable portrayal by Shakespeare. Nor was Richard's legendary disability quite

Richard III's legacy has been haunted by accusations that he had the 12-year-old King Edward murdered in the Tower of London

as pronounced as many believe: despite the nickname 'Crouchback', many now think that he suffered from little more than a routine irregularity of the shoulder. The last Yorkist, Richard was killed by Lancastrian forces headed by the future king Henry Tudor after his army deserted him at the Battle of Bosworth Field.

The Tudors

Henry VIII and Anne Boleyn – whom he would later have executed on trumped-up charges of adultery

1485–1509: Henry VII

A great manager of the royal accounts, patron of religious and educational institutions, and instigator of many grand buildings across the English nation, including the ornate perpendicular interiors of the chapels at Westminster Abbey and King's College in Cambridge.

1509–1547: Henry VIII

Of Henry's string of six serial marriages, only two were based on anything even

appropriating affection: the others were all attempts at consolidating royal clout, something which he achieved like no ruler before or after (by the end of his reign, his annual income was a then unthinkable £250,000 a year). He aided the Reformation, breaking off from the Vatican after the Pope refused to sanction his divorce from Catherine of Aragon and establishing himself at the head of the new Church of England. At the same time, he revealed an increasingly despotic character, ushering in a reign of terror against papal sympathisers and over-indulging to such an extent that, in the twilight years of his life, a complex system of pulleys was employed to hoist his grossly overweight frame onto his long-suffering horse.

1553: Lady Jane Grey

The wily Duke of Northumberland persuaded ailing King Edward VI – who died of tuberculosis aged just 15 – to will his crown to Northumberland's own daughter-in-law, Lady Jane Grey, but the plan fell apart when the rightful heir, Mary, marched on London and had herself crowned to scenes of public jubilation. The 'Nine Days Queen', as Jane later became known, was executed along with her husband on 12th February.

Lady Jane Grey was forced to become Queen by the Duke of Northumberland

1553–1558: Mary I

A devout Catholic, Mary dedicated her reign to re-establishing the authority of the Pope in England – an aim she pursued with extreme harshness, burning almost 300 Protestants in her blanket religious persecution and earning herself the nickname 'Bloody Mary' in the process. Her inability to produce an heir (the closest she came was a phantom pregnancy in 1555) all but guaranteed a return to Protestantism following her death.

Mary's attempts to re-establish a Catholic monarchy split the English nation in two

1558–1603: Elizabeth I

Elizabeth's reign saw an unprecedented flourishing of art and exploration, with new theatrical works from the likes of Marlowe and Shakespeare, a circumnavigation of the globe by Sir Francis Drake and the ongoing colonisation of the New World by Sir Walter Raleigh.

Her rallying speech before the legendary defeat of the Spanish Armada ('I know I have the body of a weak and feeble woman; but I have the heart and stomach of a king, and of a king of England too!') exposed an aggressive nationalism that made her hugely popular among her people.

That said, Elizabeth failed to marry or produce an heir – some say because she was loathe to share power, or saw that by not marrying she could use her potential marriage status to useful political end; others because she was always in love with one man only: Robert Dudley, Earl of Leicester. After her death, his last letter to her was found in a casket beside her bed.

Queen Elizabeth I on her deathbed. Few women have left so powerful an imprint on British history as the 'Virgin Queen', whose iron resolve made her more popular than most kings

1603–1625: James I

James was among the most scholarly of all kings, writing many books (including one of the first anti-smoking arguments, *A Counterblaste to Tobacco*) and encouraging the arts to flourish during his reign. That said, his obvious homosexual inclinations made him unpopular with his own people ('Elizabeth was King; now James is Queen', ran a popular joke of the time). James also found himself on the wrong side of a group of radical English

King James I questions Guy Fawkes about the plot to blow up the Houses of Parliament

The Great Fire of London razed much of the city to the ground, despite Charles II's personal efforts to fight the flames

Catholics, who were famously foiled in their plot to assassinate him by blowing up the Houses of Parliament with gunpowder in 1605.

1625–1649: Charles I

Charles' untimely end was the result of years of quarrelling with Parliament, which led to a split between Royalist 'Cavaliers' and Parliamentary 'Roundheads', with Oliver Cromwell leading the latter to victory in two civil wars. The second resulted in the king's trial and subsequent beheading outside the Banqueting House in Whitehall.

1660–1685: Charles II

The eleven-year Interregnum – in which England was ruled by a Parliamentary Council – ended after Cromwell's (less effectual) son abdicated, and the subsequent general election resulted in a Royalist victory and Charles II's restoration to the throne. His reign was marked by both the Great Plague (1665) and the Great Fire of London (1666), the latter of which saw him personally fighting the flames at one point. Rumoured to have been a secret Catholic for much of his life, Charles finally converted on his deathbed.

1685–1688: James II

Openly Catholic, James was forcibly deposed in 1688 after the birth of his son threatened a Roman Catholic succession. While attempting to flee London for France, James threw the Great Seal of the Realm into the River Thames.

Mary II and William of Orange were crowned in 1689 – the marriage lasted five years

1689–1694: Mary II

Ruled alongside her husband, also her cousin, William of Orange. William reigned alone following Mary's passing until his own death, in 1702 – the result of a fall from his horse, which had apparently tripped on a large molehill. His detractors took to toasting the 'little gentleman in black velvet' for many years after.

1702–1714: Anne

Despite no fewer than 18 pregnancies, only one of Anne's children survived infancy, dying aged 11. Subsequent depression and ongoing illness caused her to over-indulge in food and drink (her fondness for brandy earned her the nickname 'Brandy Nan'), and she became so overweight in her later years that a system of chairs and pulleys was employed to hoist her around. Following heirless Anne's death from gout (after which her body was so swollen that it was buried in an almost cubic coffin), the Act of Settlement handed the throne over to Electress Sophia of Hanover, granddaughter of James I, thus beginning the line of Hanoverian monarchs that continues to this day.

Anne's later years were blighted by depression and overeating

1714–1727: George I

Arriving in England with two mistresses (nicknamed 'the Maypole' and 'the Elephant', for obvious reasons) and only the most rudimentary grasp of English, George was an incongruous and uneasy ruler, failing spectacularly to establish a relationship with his English subjects and leaving the majority of administrative responsibilities to Robert Walpole, England's first Prime Minister.

George I took no active interest in ruling England – most likely because he was so homesick for his German homeland

1727–1760: George II

George II resembled his father not only physically, but also in his deep-seated dislike for the English way of life ('the Devil take the whole island') and strained relationship with his eldest son, Frederick, at whose death (from being hit in the head with a cricket ball) the king was barely able to suppress his pleasure. George also suffered an inglorious end, dying while overstraining himself in the toilet at Kensington Palace.

1760–1820: George III

George's legendary insanity was most likely due to a blood condition known as porphyria, although some blame poisoning by arsenic. Regardless of its root, the illness caused the king to talk nonsense for hours or even days on end – often to imaginary characters, some of them 'angels' – and eventually led to him being locked away in Windsor Castle in 1811. By the time he died, nine years later, he was blind, deaf and completely insane.

1820–1830: George IV

Highly oversexed, George was said to have cut a lock from the hair of every woman he engaged in intimate relationships with and placed it in an envelope with her name on it; at the time of his death, grossly obese and loathed by all but a loyal few of his subjects, there were rumoured to be 7,000 such envelopes in existence.

1830–1837: William IV

William's short reign saw a great deal of reform, including a restructuring of Parliament, with a decline in the powers of the unelected House of Lords and a surge in the influence of the more democratic House of Commons. He also oversaw the provision of social security for the nation's poor, the restriction of child labour and the abolition of slavery.

George III's declining mental health lead to him being locked away in Windsor Castle

1837–1901: Victoria

Victoria's 64-year reign is notable not only for its length, but also for its breadth; she oversaw an era of industrial expansion, with the establishment of first trains and then motor cars, not to mention the colonization of India, of which she was crowned Empress in 1877 (at its apex, the British Empire covered one fifth of the earth's surface and a quarter of its population). Morally upstanding and formal to the point of ridicule (her use of the royal 'we' was a source of constant amusement among her critics), Victoria lived a life of domestic bliss with her beloved Prince Albert, plunging into a deep depression following his early death in 1861.

The second half of Victoria's reign was a protracted period of mourning for her husband

1901–1910: Edward VII

A high-ranking Freemason, Edward attained the position of Grand Master in 1874, a role in which he regularly travelled the country to attend foundation ceremonies or open public buildings. By the end of his life, Edward had contributed more to the fraternity – both financially and in terms of his enormous public clout – than almost any member in its history.

1910–1936: George V

Best remembered for his blanket eradication of all Germanic names and titles following the outbreak of the First World War: his cousin Prince Louis of Battenberg, for example, became Louis Mountbatten, while the name of the royal house itself was changed from 'Saxe-Coburg-Gotha' to the decidedly more British-sounding 'Windsor' – a name it retains to this day.

1936: Edward VIII

Following his death, the British public had high hopes for George's immediate heir,

George V rewrote the Germanic heritage of the Royal Family and adopted the more British-sounding surname 'Windsor'

his dashing and socially outgoing eldest son Edward VIII, but the young king was never actually crowned. Instead, to the country's shock, Edward actually abdicated so that he could marry his common sweetheart, the twice-married American actress Mrs Wallis Simpson, bringing the monarchy to the verge of collapse in the process.

George VI inspects a bombed-out London house during the Blitz. The bombing of the palace had brought him much closer to his people

regularly visiting the bombed-out homes of families affected by the Blitz.

1952 – : Elizabeth II

As one of history's longest-reigning monarchs, Elizabeth II has seen both the highs and lows of royal public relations, ultimately keeping a place in the hearts of her people through an endearing mix of conservative values, a wry sense of humour and a trademark taste in colourful overcoats and hats.

1936–1952: George VI

George VI never looked as if he was made of stuff stern enough to withstand the slings and arrows of kingship, but when his brother Edward abdicated, he more than rose to the challenge. Shy to the point of awkwardness (he suffered from a severe stammer – largely tempered in later life – that made public speaking a painful ordeal), George nevertheless became a much loved ruler during the Second World War, during which he and his wife Elizabeth, the late Queen Mother, remained in London,

Her marriage to the Duke of Edinburgh – her second cousin once removed – has remained strong despite initial objections by her mother (who referred to him as 'the Hun' due to the fact that his sisters married Nazi supporters). Her relationship with Lady Diana Spencer, however, was reputedly cold from the first and her initial failure to grieve publicly for the princess following her death in 1997 led to

Elizabeth being vilified by the national press. She also refused to acknowledge the subsequent relationship between Prince Charles and Camilla Parker-Bowles, although her attitude towards them softened in the wake of their marriage.

If her relationships with other royals have been stormy, Elizabeth has always enjoyed a talent for getting on with various world leaders – Jacques Chirac, for example, is allowed to substitute the obligatory French wine for beer at formal Buckingham Palace dinners.

There can be no doubt that of late, the monarchy has had to listen to public opinion: gone are the days of the divine right of kings to rule and roister as they see fit. It was a lesson hard learnt, but well learnt, by a family born to privilege, but also lifetimes of responsibility and scrutiny.

A formal portrait of the royal couple. Despite turbulent times, Elizabeth remains firmly in the hearts of her people

Picture Credits